The Collector's Guide to

THIMBLES

AUTHOR'S NOTE

The pictures in this book have been assembled over a period of ten years—taken either by me on my travels around the world, or supplied by friends and colleagues in the thimble community. Many thimbles are extremely rare, and some photographs had to be taken very quickly in extremely poor conditions. It would be impossible now to reassemble all the important thimbles recorded here, or even to locate many that may have disappeared from the scene or changed hands from collector to collector. It has therefore been decided, in the interest of all thimble collectors who will read this book, to include among the vast majority of photographs of excellent quality, a few pictures of a slightly lower standard than I would normally have wished, on the understanding that, although we intend the book to be as attractive as possible, the principle concern of the work is to give all collectors as thorough and comprehensive a grounding as possible in the broadest range of material available.

The Collector's Guide to

THIMBLES

BRIDGET McCONNEL

BRACKEN BOOKS

WEST GRID STAMP					
NN		RR		WW	
NT		RT	6/95	WO	
NC		RC	11/99	WL	
NH		RB		WM	
NL		RP		WT	
NV		RS		WA	
NM		RW		WR	
NB		RV		WS	
NE					
NP					

PUBLISHER'S NOTE

Prices for thimbles sold at specific auctions are given in the local
currency with the date of sale; where there is more than one
thimble in a single image the reader should read the dimensions
and prices from left to right. All other prices mentioned are given
in £ sterling followed by US$ in brackets; the exchange rate has
been calculated at £1 to US$1.65.

CONTENTS

INTRODUCTION

Thimbles have been made from an enormous

variety of materials and in a range of styles

that reflect the period of manufacture and

country of origin. Building a collection that

has breadth, substance and personal interest

presents an exciting and rewarding challenge

to the thimble collector.

Thimbles have been in continuous use around the world for some 2000 years in one form or another. Their use by virtually every known civilization, combined with the enormous variety of materials that they are made from, and the delicacy and beauty of their design make them one of the most fascinating and popular of all collectable items.

The word 'thimble' is of uncertain origin, but derives from the medieval English *thymel*, or *thuma*—meaning thumb. It is unlikely though that the early thimble was worn only on the thumb which, itself, means thick finger. The etymological roots of the word 'thumb' lie close to the Latin *tumere*, to swell. A finger with a thimble on it is thickened and resembles a thumb. Curiously, in other European languages, the word for thimble is related much more closely to the finger than the thumb.

Thimbles have been fashioned in stone, wood, horn, glass, bone, tortoiseshell, leather, bronze, porcelain, gold, silver, ivory, mother-of-pearl and many other materials and metal alloys. Given the diversity of materials, nationalities, periods and designs, both new and more established collectors can have serious problems in building a sensibly organized, and thus more interesting, collection. An additional pitfall is the use of antique moulds to reproduce old thimbles complete with the original hallmarks. While these may not have been created to deceive in the first instance, these reproductions may occasionally be presented as genuine antiques. Equally, crude workmanship is not necessarily an indication of antiquity: rough hand-produced thimbles are still being made today, while fine, intricate examples may be many centuries old.

This book has been devised to provide the advice and expertise that will allow collectors at all levels of experience to fight their way through the existing morass of information. Building a collection that has breadth, substance, and character can take a considerable amount of research and perseverance, so *A Collector's Guide To Thimbles* advises on research, cataloguing, maintenance, and display—allowing a collection to be assembled, preserved and presented to full advantage. Information on dealing, auctions, and general buying and selling, with appropriate price guidance should enable even beginners to trade their thimbles with greater confidence.

It should be noted that prices vary according to condition, availability and, in a few popular cases, fashion. The prices given in this book are those that thimbles have actually realized.

The thimble was developed to protect the finger while a needle was pushed against it through a variety of materials. Two distinct types of thimbles (and needles) developed: the coarser models for heavier industrial work (worn mainly by men for tasks such as sail-making); and more delicate versions for finer work. The earliest form of pusher, made of stone, was probably held in the palm of the hand, much in the manner of a sailor's palm (a leather or canvas pad,

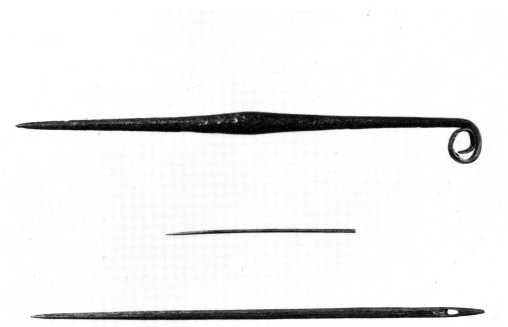

Left: *A bronze hairpin, a fine silver needle and a bronze bodkin found in a Naqada tomb, Egypt. They date from the pre-dynastic period before 3000BC. The end of the fine silver needle has been broken off and the fine eye is not visible here.*

often with a reinforced metal disc in the middle, the disc pitted in order to hold the needle still while pressure is exerted using the whole arm). Thimble development always followed needle development, responding to refinements in needle design as they were adopted for different uses. However, once needles were strong enough to withstand the pressure of being pushed against a metal (bronze, iron, or steel) thimble, and could cope with the even greater stresses that could be exerted from the side rather than the top of the finger (a technique necessary when working with heavier materials), ring-shaped ('open top') thimbles, which were also much easier to make, began to appear. Some tailors' thimbles today are still open top. The evolving thimble eventually took on the form of a small bell-shaped cap worn on the first or middle finger, reaching down to the first joint: this shape remains with us today.

A knowledge of the history of the development of the thimble and needle will help you to identify the major changes in thimble design over the centuries, and will increase your awareness of periods and dates. Examples of the most important thimble types have been included to indicate landmarks in the development of design and the progression of technical ingenuity. As you familiarize yourself with the changing shapes and styles of thimbles, you will gain confidence in your ability to authenticate and date both your own and other people's collections. Much of the time, dating thimbles is an approximate affair, depending on well-informed guesswork: new research and discoveries may sometimes disturb long-established beliefs about a particular item in your collection. Even if this upsets or unbalances your collection, it must be accepted with good grace: it should not deter you from attempting to date your other pieces—and remember

that new information may just as often indicate that one of your less prized pieces is much more significant than you had imagined.

DATING YOUR COLLECTION

In many cases the dating of an unattributed thimble has to rest on a knowledge of where it was found and of its consequent probable connections, and a comparison with the shapes and designs of other artefacts of the same period. Inevitably this means that many thimbles are simply cited as circa (*c.*) meaning 'around a given date'.

Dating pieces by relying on one particular motif, design or style alone can be dangerous and misleading. Many of the most popular motifs have been in use over hundreds, even thousands of years and have been repeatedly re-interpreted. Honeysuckle, for example, was a favourite of the ancient Egyptians; it recurs in medieval and Renaissance designs and it resurfaces once more as a motif used on nineteenth-century thimbles, when it is sometimes described as a 'palmette'. Similarly, the strapwork introduced by the Huguenots into English seventeenth-century silver designs echoed earlier, Byzantine, design devices.

A SHORT HISTORY OF NEEDLES AND THIMBLES

The earliest example of sewn work appears on the clothing of a Cro-Magnon man (*c.*30,000 BC), dug up in Vladimir, Russia, whose fur cap and boots are decorated with ivory beads. The earliest needles to be found so far are Neolithic bone needles taken from caves in France, dating from *c.*15,000 BC. An indication of the tools used to make and decorate garments of this time is provided by an example of a Neolithic needle pusher made in stone. Dating from *c.*10,000 BC,

Right: *Two pre-dynastic Egyptian gold needles. The eyes and points of both needles are intact. The ancient Egyptians mixed arsenic into the gold to give it greater tensile strength.*

pushers with grooves have been found in Neolithic sites as far apart as Europe, Africa and China, and would have been held in the palm of the hand. Bones, porcupine quills, and wood are the most likely materials to have been used for needles, as it would have been difficult to drill a fine eye into stone and other hard substances.

By 5000 BC, there was a thriving weaving and sewing industry along the Nile valley producing goods in linen from flax, sewn with spun thread. An ancient hybrid pressure tool, made from stone and dating from 1200–1000 BC, was excavated from the Nile valley (it can now be seen in the Metropolitan Museum of Art, New York). It must have been used in leather work or for the piercing of heavy materials with an awl and not with the short gold needles made to sew the embroidery spun from fine linen thread. The Egyptians are known to have been using iron, bronze, silver, and gold needles at least as early as 3000 BC.

China also produced fine silk thread from 2000 BC onwards, and consequently fine needles must also have existed—though none has survived. However, the earliest thimble yet found is Chinese, taken from the tomb of a minor court official of the Han Dynasty (206 BC–220AD). An open top example, it is made of iron (or a type of steel) and was found as part of a complete sewing set.

Trade along the extensive silk routes spread the Chinese knowledge and mastery of steel-working to Asia Minor. The famous Damascus steel industry exported its distinctive Damascene work from *c*.200 BC, although as yet no early sewing implements have been found. Bronze *acutrudia* (held in the palm of the hand to push bodkins or awls through the material being worked) date from *c*.100 BC to as late as the seventeenth century in some places.

The oldest European thimbles yet discovered were found in the Byzantine sections of Corinth. These thimbles date from the ninth and tenth centuries and are contemporary with the more commonly found earliest Turko-Slavic (Islamic) thimbles made in cast bronze which date from the tenth to the sixteenth centuries. Thimbles have also been found in Cordoba, Spain; these may date from the Moorish occupation of the southern third of Spain from any time between the eighth and fifteenth centuries. Examples of these Hispano-Moresque thimbles can be seen in the archaeological museum in Madrid, and they were probably used for heavy work such as carpet-making, saddlery or sail-making. Small round thimbles have been found in many sites in Asia Minor, and some historians suggest that they may have been brought back by Crusaders and subsequently directly influenced the design of the rounded medieval European thimble.

By the mid-fourteenth century, plain medieval bronze or brass thimbles, made by casting or hammering, were common in Europe. The acorn-shaped cap that is typical of the time is fairly shallow, and sometimes has a hole in its top (this may have been for ventilation, or may mark the point at which it was held as it was removed from its cast). These medieval thimbles are delicate enough for embroidery—and fine spun thread was by now readily available—although fine needles were costly. During the fifteenth century,

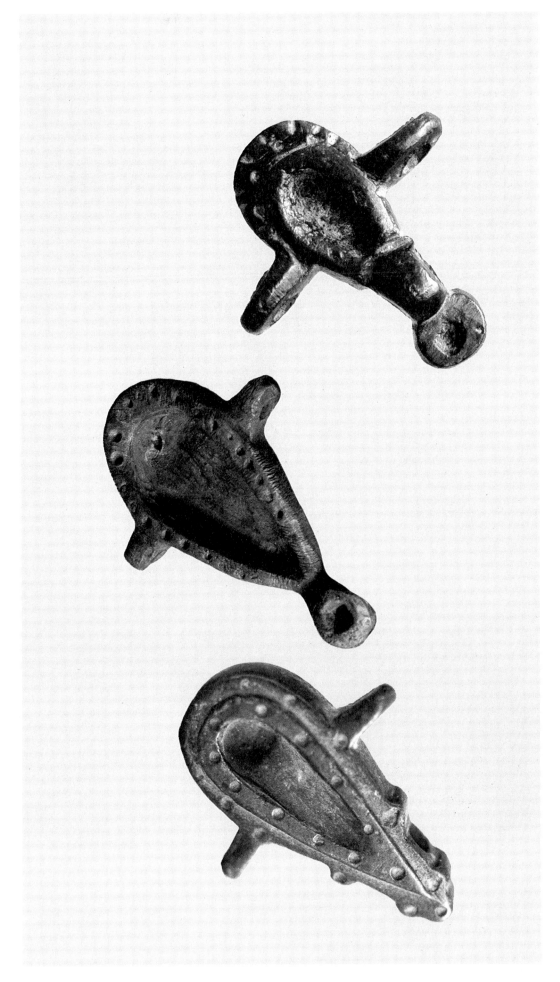

Left: *A selection of bronze palm pushers or acutrudia. They are made of bronze or brass and date from the 11th to the 15th centuries. These were found in Turkey and the Middle East.*

Right: *A brass 15th-century European thimble. Note the domed top and the spiral pattern of hand punches. It is slightly taller than the earlier acorn-top thimbles.*

brass thimbles continued to be cast in a mould or hammered but became slightly deeper in shape.

However it was the development of the Nuremberg thimble in the early sixteenth century that marked the turning point in European thimble production. In 1530, Nuremberg thimble-makers discovered a superior metal alloy, made of copper and zinc, which created a smooth, bright brass of an even texture. The Nuremberg craftsmen also produced gold and silver thimbles (as well as fine steel needles) in quantity. These are among the earliest thimbles to be decorated and some bear inscriptions: makers' marks are sometimes found at the start of the knurled indentations.

In England, fine needle-makers established a factory in Long Crendon, Buckinghamshire, in 1650, and a London needle factory was set up in Threadneedle Street—hence the name. English seventeenth-century thimbles are very distinctive, recognizable by their domed tops, straight sides and tall slim shape. They were made in brass, silver and gold and were often decorated with a form of strapwork. Some bear religious mottoes around the bottom rim, and the indentations appear as square waffles or tiny circles. One of the most important manufacturers of brass working thimbles of the time was John Lofting, who had brought a new casting method with him from Holland in 1693, and was revolutionizing the English thimble-making industry, firstly in his factory in Islington, London, and later at a larger factory in Buckinghamshire. At the end of the seventeenth century, pinchbeck sewing items started to appear, made from an alloy of five parts copper to one part zinc; pinchbeck was invented by Christopher Pinchbeck (1670–1732) as an imitation of gold. Some pinchbeck pieces were dipped in gold ie gilded.

Eighteenth-century thimbles are more diverse, ranging from squat examples in the early and mid-1700s to straight-sided, round-topped taller versions later in the century. The indentations on thimbles changed from the waffles and circles of the seventeenth century to circles in the early eighteenth century, and to dots (still with us) at the end of the eighteenth century. Meissen started producing porcelain thimbles c.1720 and squat filigree silver thimbles were also introduced in the early years of the century. Reinforced steel-topped silver thimbles were being produced, as were enamelled examples from the English south Staffordshire factories, notably from the area around the town of Bilston, towards the end of the century.

The elegance of general design prevalent at the end of the eighteenth century was reflected in the work of thimble-makers. Thimbles had become taller, and had assumed a beehive shape. A popular development at the end of the eighteenth century and the beginning of the nineteenth century was the 'toy' thimble containing a tiny scent bottle. Such thimbles were made of gold, silver or pinchbeck; some examples are decorated with filigree, while others consist of engraved or enamelled decoration on a plain body. The bottle would probably have contained scent or scented oil used to stop fine steel pins or needles from rusting. The bottle was attached to the thimble by an interior thread in its rim. This screwed on to the base, which was additionally engraved with a seal showing the owner's initials.

In 1816 the famous Piercy's patent thimble was registered by John Piercy, an English craftsman. His thimbles were made of tortoiseshell embellished with gold or silver, and most featured a shield flanked by a lion and a unicorn. Many versions of this thimble were produced, and on several the shield has been applied crookedly—this does not mean that it has been damaged.

A distinctive wooden thimble of the time is the Tunbridge ware thimble. This sometimes came with its own matching case and was produced by companies such as the George Wise Turnery, c.1830.

The most famous mother-of-pearl thimbles from the early to mid-nineteenth century came from France. Most were made by artists living and working in the Palais Royal district of Paris and are distinguished by a central oval enamel plaque bearing a pansy or a tiny flower. As the century progressed, the shape of the mother-of-pearl thimbles changed—the beehive shape was typical at the turn of the century while by 1850 the flat top had become fashionable. Most of the thimbles were made from a single piece of shell and were banded in gilt metal; some bore a tiny gold shield in the middle. Silver thimbles of this period tended to be taller and slimmer with richly decorated borders.

Placing your thimbles in a relevant social and artistic context will often help to date them and trace their origins. It is for this reason that commemorative

A Chronology of Thimbles

1 Han dynasty bronze sewing rings.

2 11th century Byzantine bronze or brass sewing rings.

3 Hispano-Moresque, bronze, 12th–15th centuries (left). Turko-Slavic, bronze, 12th–15th centuries (right).

4 Roundtop or Levantine thimbles, bronze or brass, 12th–13th centuries.

5 Two 14th-century European, bronze or brass,

6 Early 16th-century European, brass, makers' marks appear.

7 Mid 16th century, brass, Nuremberg.

8 Mid 17th century, silver, English Commonwealth (left). Late 17th century (top right). John Lofting style, brass, (lower right).

9 Stubby shaped early 18th-century English, silver filigree work (top left). Brass working style (lower left). Taller domed top, European, end of the 18th century (right).

10 Early 19th-century beehive shape, European.

11 The taller mid 19th-century British shape.

12 Silver thimble, British, late 19th- century.

INTRODUCTION

thimbles are enduringly popular, as it is delightful to recreate the scene in your imagination, when, for example, confronted by a thimble celebrating the great Exhibition at London's Crystal Palace in 1851.

Investigating the needlework current at the time a thimble was made will also improve your understanding of its design and construction. For example, fine work requires fine tools, and it is therefore clear that a large heavy iron thimble of the Byzantine era would not have been used for delicate embroidery of the same date. Many categories of thimble have still to be discovered, as it is apparent that there would always have been a variety of thimbles, each related and suited to needlework of a particular kind.

A SHORT HISTORY OF NEEDLEWORK

The earliest pieces of delicate stitching that have survived date from c.5000 BC and were found in ancient Egyptian tombs. The linen cloth, made from flax, is of fine quality and would have been sewn with fine needles; bodkins (used for holing or threading when working thicker materials) of wood, bone, copper, silver, bronze and gold have also been recovered. Products of the Persian and Babylonian civilizations in existence in c.3000 BC have also survived. The Babylonians are believed to have invented gold-work around that time using spun gold thread, a technique which the Egyptians were later to develop further.

Fragments of Egyptian tapestry embroidered with fine thread on a linen cloth (now in the Egyptian Museum, Cairo) date from c.1550 BC and employ some of the Egyptians' favourite design motifs. These included the lotus flower, egg and dart designs, rushes, and the leaves and blossom of the honeysuckle. Expensive gold thread was used for the most prestigious pieces of work, whereas gilded cat gut was employed as a less expensive alternative, for instance in the work decorating Solomon's temple.

By the first century AD, the art of embroidery was so sophisticated that Virgil was moved to describe it as 'painting with the needle'. From the first to the fourth centuries, Rome produced much embroidery done in purple wool on linen. Indigo was the most expensive dye and purple therefore became the colour associated with the Emperors and the aristocracy. The most common motifs in their embroidery were human figures, animals and foliage, particularly trailing vines. By the end of the fifth century, Egypt was exporting embroidery incorporating Christian symbols and scenes from the Gospels. Byzantium, too, was famed for the needlework it was producing during this period.

By the tenth century, Sicily had succeeded Byzantium as a leading centre of art and exported the Arabic designs so typical of the pre-Norman period in that region. In England, the art of embroidery flowered between 1250 and 1350, when the Embroiderers' Guild was established, giving rise to a body of work known as the *Opus Anglicanum*. The Syon Cope in the British Museum is a fine example of the standards of the time. A large proportion of the most beautiful English embroidery of this period was designed by monks who otherwise specialized in illuminating manuscripts. The actual sewing was done mainly by women though.

Italian embroidery flourished in the fourteenth century, particularly in Florence. Francesco Squarcione, founder of the Paduan school of painting, was especially renowned for his work in embroidery design—it was common, principally in Italy, for tapestry and embroidery designs ('cartoons') to be produced by painters during this period.

Perhaps the most attractive shaded gold-work ever produced emerged from the rich courts of the Dukes of Burgundy, based in Flanders in the fifteenth century. Known as *or nu* (naked gold), the tradition of rich embroidery work expanded during the following two centuries and influenced fashions at all the European courts. Precious stones and brightly coloured intricate designs of flowers and foliage, often using black silk thread on linen, were widely employed on both clothes and domestic items, such as cross-stitch samplers and boxes covered with padded stumpwork.

Petit point, the finest form of tapestry, was widespread in seventeenth-century France, and by the eighteenth century, enormous quantities of needlework were being made throughout Europe, including wall-hangings, clothes, samplers, and silk pictures (landscapes among them). The focus of English embroidery had also become domestic and courtly rather than ecclesiastical, following the Reformation and the dissolution of the monasteries. The declining production and disappearance of many of the skills associated with the sewing of ecclesiastical embroidery were only finally arrested in England in the nineteenth century when the resurgence of the High Church and the consequent demand for greater ecclesiastical ornamentation promoted the revival of decorative embroidery on vestments, pew seats and other church furnishings.

This trend was regrettably reversed again when the invention of the sewing machine, both domestic and commercial, initiated another decline in embroidery standards. The long-taught skills of domestic needlework, exemplified above all in the delicate and often touching samplers of young girls, have since radically deteriorated.

A brighter note to finish on is today's renewed interest in sewing in its social context. Perhaps the isolation provoked by television is being challenged by the ever-growing popularity of quilting, for example in the United States, and lace-making groups in Europe. The lace bobbin, the tatting shuttle, the needle and the thimble are not valued just for the work they are instrumental in, but also for their role in encouraging the binding together of, and the exchange of information between communities.

EARLY MEDIEVAL AND FIFTEENTH-CENTURY THIMBLES

The oldest thimbles in most collections are made

from bronze and are quite crude in design. The

Moorish influence can clearly be seen in

Hispano-Moresque and Turko-Slavic thimbles.

Medieval thimbles are the earliest thimbles that are really accessible to the individual collector. The first thimbles known to have been used in Britain and Europe date from the fourteenth century. Sometimes referred to as 'skeps' or 'acorn tops', they were made from brass, copper and bronze. These thimbles are difficult to date with accuracy or confidence: the quality and composition of the metal alloys varied enormously. Even museums are very cautious about metal-testing as a means of establishing a precise date. In addition, if tools are served very well by their shape, this can change very little over timescales of hundreds of years; the shape of an object therefore is not in itself necessarily a good guide to the date of an object.

Until the sixteenth century, metal thimbles were either cast or hammered into a die (mould). Indentations were hand-punched in an orderly fashion, starting from the open end and finishing short of the crown (or top), like a monk's tonsure. The bare crown on the thimble top disappeared with the emergence of the Nuremberg thimbles in the sixteenth century. Some acorn-tops show the pleats characteristic of metal thimbles in which the metal cooled too much before it had been adequately hammered.

Left: *A tailor's ring, bronze or brass, 11th–15th centuries. It is similar in style to those found in the Byzantine section of Corinth.*

Left: *A brass or bronze English thimble, mid 14th century. The hand punches run vertically up the sides of the thimble and in concentric circles over the top.*

Right: *Brass thimbles, English, late 14th century. They are known as skeps or acorn tops. These thimbles show a variety of hand punches and 'tonsures' or plain tops and single incized lines round their bases. Four of them have holes.*

Makers' marks such as a rowel (spur), dagger, flower or keys can sometimes be seen at the beginning of the indentations. Unfortunately these remain undocumented, although they are thought to have been introduced *c.*1530. Apart from an incised line, very little decoration on thimbles is apparent until the sixteenth century.

The strong Moorish influence following the Crusades is very evident. Examples of both closed-topped Hispano-Moresque and Turko-Slavic (also known as Islamic or onion top) thimbles, dating from the tenth to the sixteenth centuries are numerous. The round-topped Levant thimbles are rarer.

It is assumed that the ring type (or open top) thimble must have evolved before the closed top; in fact both shapes had been used for many centuries in tandem, the ring type for heavy work and the closed top for more delicate, intricate embroidery. Although ornamental or decorative thimbles appear very early in history, both Hispano-Moresque and Turko-Slavic thimbles clearly fall into the heavy working thimble category. It is almost certain that more delicate thimbles for use with finer cloth were made then, but none of these has yet been found.

HISPANO-MORESQUE THIMBLES

Hispano-Moresque thimbles have been dated to the twelfth to fifteenth centuries. They were cast in one piece and their distinctive pointed shape bears a close resemblance to the shape of Moorish soldiers' helmets. These thimbles have been found in Cordoba, Spain, at a site with other objects of a similar period. One such example is signed in Arabic 'made by Al-Sayib'.

Cordoba became renowned for steel-working during the Moorish occupation of southern Spain from the eighth to the fifteenth centuries. The fine steel needles produced there were extremely costly—even an affluent woman would rarely have been able to afford more than one at a time.

Hispano-Moresque thimbles have no rims but some of them have decorated borders. They are heavy and approximately 2in (5cm) high. The indentations punched around the side stop short of the top and are large and round; this implies that these thimbles were made for use with thick needles and that they were probably used in saddlery or rug work. Thimbles made in two sections—the cap placed on a cylinder and joined to it with a seam—did not appear until the sixteenth century.

Right: *Three bronze thimbles, Hispano-Moresque. The shape of these thimbles probably changed relatively little between the 12th and 15th centuries, so well adapted were they for their particular tasks. They may have been used in sail-making, embroidery on rugs or sewing bales for transport. They have attractive decorated borders and distinctive pointed tops.*

Above: *Five bronze thimbles from Asia Minor, Hispano-Moresque. The two thimbles at the outer edges of the picture are more rustic in character and although not* *necessarily earlier in date may have been made in a less sophisticated metal-working region. Some of them have the same bare tonsures as the English acorn-tops.*

TURKO-SLAVIC (ISLAMIC) THIMBLES

The second style of early thimble is known as the Turko-Slavic or onion top thimble. These have been found in Asia Minor across the Balkans to Eastern Europe and are thought to date from as early as the thirteenth century. The typical bulbous top is reminiscent of the domes of mosques and Byzantine churches.

Like the Hispano-Moresque thimbles, they are made of cast bronze and have neat hand-punched indentations stopping short of the top. Some tops are decorated with three or four holes. Border ornaments include turned rings, a small lip or a broad decorated band. These thimbles are generally about 2½in (7cm) high; their diameters vary—the larger ones were obviously designed for men and the smaller for women —but they are all very solidly constructed. It has been suggested that the onion-shaped end would originally have been padded inside, making it easier to use; otherwise the tip of the finger had nothing to press against in order to direct the needle. All of the known examples are working thimbles and were also probably used for rugs, leather, or sewing up bales for transport.

Above and right above: *Four bronze or brass thimbles, Turko-Slavic, 13th–17th centuries. The two on the left are more sophisticated in having an* *onion-top shape and a narrower base. The tops may have been padded inside. The two on the right have bare tonsures.*

Right: *A bronze or brass thimble, Levantine, 9th–11th centuries. Modern European thimbles most closely resemble these of all the thimbles dating from this period and found in the Middle East.*

Right: *A brass thimble, Levantine, 9th–11th centuries. This thimble and the one above are decorated with a cross running up the sides and over the top.*

Above: *Two bronze or brass thimbles, Levantine, 9th–11th centuries. The pronounced rims are curiously characteristic of much later European thimbles.*

some are decorated with a chevron motif curving from one side of the thimble to the other, or a cross (as on a hot cross bun) on top.

Fine embroidery was certainly being produced in centres of Arabic influence such as Sicily, then ruled by Norman kings, and in the Norman-dominated cities of the Levant. This half-Christian, half-Muslim world enjoyed luxury and refinement, and it seems probable that more delicate thimbles than those discovered to date also existed, both in bronze and, perhaps, in precious metals.

The design motifs on these three main types of thimble show considerable variety. Some Hispano-Moresque thimbles carried small diamond-shaped motifs, and occasionally a curling vine. (The vine motif had been extensively used by Roman designers and reappears in many revivals of the Classical style. It is also a characteristic design on American thimbles of the late nineteenth and early twentieth centuries). Turko-Slavic thimbles are sometimes decorated with geometric motifs around the border and star-shaped motifs or pierced holes on top. The Levantine thimble is the only one of the three to bear a chevron or cross. The chevron had been a popular design in heraldry from the eleventh century onwards, although it appears far earlier as an Egyptian ornament and on the tomb of King Agamemnon in Greece.

It is important to remember that in the turbulent Middle Ages especially, plate (as used in its old sense to mean silver and gold) was one of the most convenient means of securing and storing personal wealth. Household plate was transportable in times of war, and was easily melted down in times of financial crisis. Although plenty of objects were made in plate, relatively few small gold and silver sewing artefacts made before the middle of the seventeenth century exist today in their original form. Bronze thimbles have lasted longer and survived intact in greater quantity primarily because more of them were made but also because their intrinsic value was very much lower.

Another material widely used in the Middle Ages was *cuir bouilli* (boiled leather). Boiled leather is almost impenetrable and its availability and price would certainly have made it an ideal material from which to make tough thimbles. (Boiled leather was also part of the protective inner wear worn with armour of the era.)

ABBASID-LEVANTINE THIMBLES

Abbasid-Levantine thimbles derive their name from their discovery in the Levant, near Baghdad, the centre of the Abbasid culture. John von Hoelle (who named them) dates them from the ninth to twelfth centuries and suggests that they may have been the forerunners of the thimbles we know today, introduced into Europe by the returning Crusaders. Smaller than the Hispano-Moresque and Turko-Slavic thimbles, with a rounder shape and a definite rim,

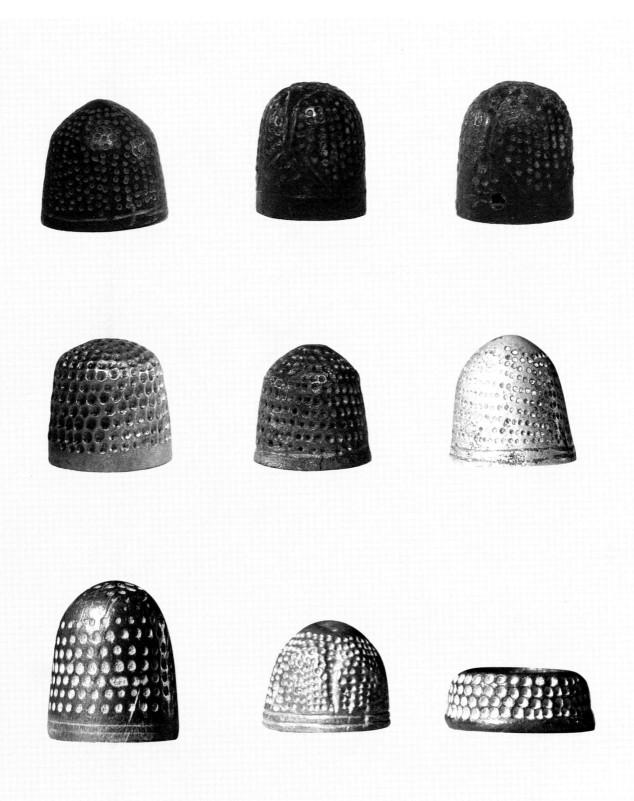

Above: *Two brass thimbles (top middle, and top right),*
Levantine, 11th–15th centuries. They are slightly taller
but have a similar chevron design to the earlier Levantine
thimbles. The other thimbles shown are brass and bronze,
European, 15th century. One of them is an open-top
sewing ring (bottom, right).

Right: *Three brass European thimbles, 15th century. The punches are more regular and open and this indicates that they may have been used with a larger coarser needle. They have tonsure tops and are still rimless.*

Above: *Two brass open-topped European sewing rings, 15th century. The ring on the left has D-shaped punches and a raised top edge, perhaps to stop the needle from slipping. The ring on the right is more crudely fashioned, with large punches for use with a coarse needle. Its waisted design may also have helped to stop the needle from slipping.*

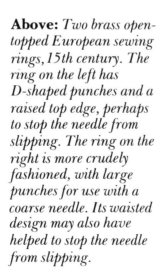

Above: *A fine group of thimbles, illustrating a wide range of sizes, shapes and designs.*

SIXTEENTH-CENTURY THIMBLES

By the sixteenth century, thimble makers were no longer the only source of these practical objects. As decoration became more elaborate, silversmiths, too, began manufacturing thimbles; these were initially meant for practical purposes, but by the end of the century, beautiful trinkets, known as toys, were growing in popularity.

The sixteenth century was one of great expansion into new worlds, of explorers, and of flamboyant confidence in the decorative arts. Although the great European ecclesiastical tradition of embroidery had faltered (in England at least because of the Reformation and the dissolution of the monasteries), needleworking skills turned to more secular and domestic purposes. Gold-thread embroidered clothes, fine linen, wall hangings and rich textiles were all common in the homes of the rich. Elizabeth I of England presented a thimble that had sides richly encrusted with precious stones to one of her ladies-in-waiting: not a very practical object perhaps, but such a gift shows the importance of needlework at the time.

Until the end of the fifteenth century, German silver mines had been the main source of silver in Europe, and proximity had therefore encouraged German craftsmen into acquiring exceptional silversmithing skills. However, these mines were almost exhausted by the sixteenth century and Europe increasingly looked for its supplies to the new silver mines being

Left: *A brass English thimble, early 16th century. It was probably cast and made in one piece. It shows the maker's mark at the base of the spiral of punches. £90.*

discovered by the Spanish in South and Central America. As a consequence of the greater diversity of sources, silver became more widely available than ever before in a variety of countries, allowing other craftsmen all over Europe to develop their own traditions in silver-working and its associated arts.

Silver thimbles were subsequently made by two types of craftsmen: silversmiths who wished to add a new item to their range of wares or who had received a special commission, and specialist thimble-makers who wanted to apply their existing metal-working skills to a new medium.

A fine example of a silver thimble made by a silversmith at this time is on view at the Metropolitan Museum of Art in New York. It consists of two parts, has a Renaissance design of racing hounds and is dated 1577. One of the most renowned craftsmen to make and design thimbles was the German John Theo de Bry, who worked in Frankfurt between 1528 and 1598, as a designer for metal engravers. Some of his work

Jon Theo de Bry

The engravings on the right on the subject of love include the inscriptions 'Beauté sans bonté ne vaut rien', 'Beauty without goodness is not worth anything' and 'Craint et amour font vivre en grand honneur', 'Belief and love lead to a life of great honour'. The thimble in the lower engraving shows a scene from the Annunciation.

Left and left below: *Two 16th-century German brass open-topped sewing rings. One of these has far cruder punches than the other.*

Above: *Two 16th-century European brass thimbles. The one on the left seems to have the initials 'A.M.' around the base and a motif resembling a snake up one side laid into the hand punches; the one on the right has a cross.*

(though none of his thimbles, as none has been found) can be seen on knife handles; prints of his designs are kept in the Victoria and Albert Museum Print Room in London.

Early silver thimbles were not produced purely for decoration or ornament: in fact silver is an eminently sensible metal with which to make thimbles because it does not mark the thread (as a base metal can) and, unlike brass, will not aggravate an infection in a cut or pin-prick.

The first filigree thimbles appeared in the sixteenth century (an outer sleeve of filigree being applied over a smooth inner body) as did the early examples of toy (in its original sense of meaning miniature trinket) thimbles. These date mostly from the end of the century and were intended as delightful gifts rather than as practical sewing accessories. They were made of two parts, with a removable cap; a shield concealed inside the cap bore the date of manufacture and the owner's initials carved under crystal. Their sides were decorated with formal medallions, quatrefoils and scrolls.

Above and left: *Two 16th-century German brass thimbles from Nuremberg, one of them taller and slimmer with a flat top and a decorative border with a fleur de lys design, the other with a decorative border of small medallions. These sold in 1989 for £200 each.*

NUREMBERG THIMBLES

The most important of all thimble-making centres at this time was to be found in Nuremberg. They had been well established in the fifteenth century but it was not until the middle and late sixteenth century that they really grew to dominate the industry. They made base and precious metal—silver—thimbles. Their success was founded on two inventions—the discovery of a better 'recipe' for brass and a technique that allowed them to make thimbles from two parts. They were able to apply patterns to flat sheets of metal which were then rolled up and cut into cylinders; the caps were soldered on. The technological developments made in the first quarter of the sixteenth cen-

tury c.1530 in founding (the process of making sheets of metal of uniform thickness, colour and consistent quality) permitted by the more efficacious combinations of copper and other metals facilitated the production of a beautiful, light, bright almost gold-like brass, which was both popular and easier to work.

The significance of the production of consistent high-quality sheet metal is hard to over-estimate; in 1537, specialist sheet metal thimble-makers broke away from the Coppersmiths Guild to form their own guild.

European metal thimbles up to this time had been manufactured in two ways: by the simplest of all metal-working techniques, the alternate heating and hammering (annealing) of thin sheets of metal into shape; and by casting (pouring molten metal into moulds). The earliest thimble-making method of all had been simply to hammer thimbles into moulds; the thimbles so made are, not surprisingly very crude compared to the work of the Nuremberg thimble-makers.

Left: *A 16th-century German brass thimble. It follows the shorter squat design and has a pointed top. Valued in 1989 at £120.*

Right: *Two 16th-century German brass thimbles from Nuremberg. The one on the left is shorter with a pointed top and was made from two parts: the one on the right is open-topped.*

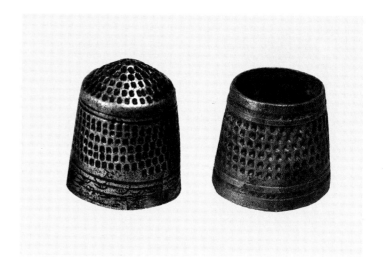

The thinner, more regular sheets of metal at the disposal of the Nuremberg craftsmen allowed them greater scope for design and decoration: taller, more elegant shapes and more intricate ornamentation became the order of the day. In the case of single-part thimbles, the basic shapes were first created from discs cut out of the thin sheet metal and heated and punched into moulds: additional patterns and knurlings were then finished by hand with finer tools, and the whole would finally be cleaned with acid and polished to a bright sheen. Two-part thimbles were cut out in exactly the same way—smaller discs were cut for the tops. The construction of these thimbles alone is therefore of little or no value in dating them. The Nuremberg thimble is, however, very distinctive: a typical specimen has a flattish top and a tall slim body, widening towards the base. The brass used looks like matt gold, with a light, delicate feel to it and the indentations are hand-punched. These indentations form a spiral, winding up the sides and continuing over the thimble's top, their fineness a sure sign that they were used with fine needles. A maker's mark—such as a clover leaf—sometimes appears at the base of the spiral: such marks are of interest, but cannot, unfortunately, be traced to individual makers. Nuremberg thimbles frequently have a decorated border of rows of small round medallions containing crosses (of Byzantine origin) around their rim. Very similar designs characterize lace ruffs of the period. The shorter, stubbier style of Nuremberg thimble, often made in two parts, had a pointed top or cap.

Various types of metal were employed in early thimble-making: they principally fall into the categories of pure copper; brass (an alloy of copper and zinc); and bronze (an alloy of copper and tin). Metal-working, and consequently thimble-making, skills naturally tended to concentrate around the areas in which the metals were mined, and a special expertise was developed in Germany, Scandinavia (particularly Sweden), and parts of Spain.

Above: *Two brass sewing rings, the one on the right inscribed 'Dio sopra el tuto'. ('God above all'), and decorated with an eagle.*

Above: *A thimble and a sewing ring, the thimble with a trefoil cut-out top and Gothic script which reads 'Avec tous . . .' (the rest is illegible), and the sewing ring of silver with a chevron design, inscribed 'Da gloriam deo'.*

SEVENTEENTH-CENTURY THIMBLES

Probably the most distinctive features of many seventeenth-century thimbles are the use of indentations shaped like waffles and of strapwork, either in a chevron form or in a 'z' shape. Another characteristic is the lack of a rim on such thimbles, which simply end with a couple of incized lines.

The seventeenth century in Europe was a period of turmoil, unceasing warfare and strife, but also one of artistic genius. Religious persecution was rampant and caused huge numbers of European craftsmen to leave their homes and seek refuge in foreign countries where they could live and work in peace. This meant an exchange of skills and ideas in the worlds of fine and decorative arts such as had never before been seen.

The Civil War in England had a marked effect on all the crafts and arts, including thimble-making. Whereas before the Civil War, silver had been widely used—albeit often gilded—in thimbles and other household items, it suffered the same fate as other metals and was frequently melted down to provide material for weapons, armour and helmets or to raise money. Most pieces that survived are, curiously, remarkable for their sloppy workmanship, clumsy construction and relatively plain appearance.

In Holland, however, Protestantism in no way cramped decorative styles. Holland's decisive victory against its Spanish enemies brought independence by

A typical mid 17th-century English Commonwealth silver thimble. It incorporates the strapwork design features shown on the adjacent contemporary textile.

SEVENTEENTH-CENTURY THIMBLES

Right: *An early 17th-century European silver thimble. The squat and stubby shape is a typical feature of many thimbles of the period. The punches follow the earlier style and are not yet arranged decoratively.*

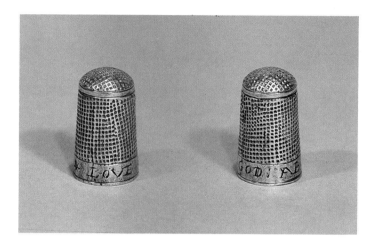

Above: *Two views of a typical mid 17th-century English Commonwealth silver thimble showing the Puritan influence in the religious motto.*

Right: *A mid 17th-century English Commonwealth silver thimble. The workmanship is rather poor; ostentatious design was frowned upon at the time.*

the middle of the century, peace and financial prosperity. Relative economic stability prevailed again after the war with England and the Civil War and fostered further technological advances. Less is known of thimble-making in Holland than in Germany, mainly because the industry was not so concentrated in individual towns and cities.

Thimble history was in the making when John Loftingh, a Dutch entrepreneur moved to England in 1688, bringing with him his new technique of brass casting. He changed his name to John Lofting, and, after an initial failed venture involving patent fire engines, concentrated his attention on thimble-making. He set up a factory in Islington, London and his breakthrough came in 1693 when he obtained a patent (Number 319) for a new casting method, previously unused in England. He later moved to Great Marlow, Buckinghamshire, where his factory, eventually powered by a water mill, was able to turn out well over 150,000 thimbles a month.

Lofting soon dominated the market—his success built on three elements. First was his personal technical knowledge of and expertise in brass casting and knurling by machine; second was his great entrepreneurial flair, especially in stealing the burgeoning American market from his Dutch rivals; and third was his insistence on quality—his thimbles are notice-

Left: *A mid 17th-century English brass thimble. The top has a clock dial design with Roman numerals.*

Above: *Two mid 17th-century English brass thimbles. They are decorated with a strapwork design, waffle-shaped punches and the two-part construction is very evident.*

Right: *A mid 17th-century English silver thimble. This is one of the first commemoratives, one oval depicting Charles II and the other Katherine of Braganza. It was probably made to celebrate their wedding in 1662. The inscription under the portrait of Charles II reads 'CRII', and that underneath Katherine 'QK'.*

Left: *A late 17th-century English brass working thimble, probably made by John Lofting. The two-part construction is obvious and it has a relatively 'factory-made' appearance. This thimble sold in 1989 for £50.*

ably better finished than those of his competitors, and are much more comfortable to use. His factory continued to trade successfully well into the eighteenth century. Lofting died in 1742.

Mid-seventeenth-century English thimbles tended to be rather crude and rudimentary, both in workmanship and design. Most thimbles had no rim, but were simply finished with one or two incised lines. They were tall and cylindrical, and were usually made in two parts. The knurlings or punches were always in patterns of waffles or small circles and strapwork (in the form of a chevron, or in a 'Z' down the thimble's side) ornamentation and clock-dial tops were also used. Mottoes were often engraved around the thimble's base, usually exhorting the user to industry ("Soe not sleeping") or alluding to the transitory nature of life. A thimble bearing the legend 'Live to die' must have been a rather depressing companion for a quiet evening's needlework.

'Matting' ornamentation made its first appearance at this time and has been in continuous use on thimbles ever since. It was originally applied to the base of

Left: *A mid 17th-century English thimble, brass with traces of silver plate. The thimble carries a strapwork design, has waffle-shaped punches and is of two-part construction with a domed top but no rim.*

Above: *A selection of mid to late 17th-century English silver thimbles. All of them have the decorative circular punches that replaced the waffle-shaped punches as the century progressed. They are generally squatter in shape than thimbles earlier in the century and most of them have personalized initials.*

Above: *A late 17th-century English silver thimble, charmingly engraved 'Do not loose me'.*

tankards and candlesticks, and comprises a series of thin engraved bands arranged to form a simple border.

Towards the end of the century, a rounder shorter thimble shape became fashionable, and the waffle motif gave way to circular patterns. Moral and religious mottoes began to disappear, but domestic platitudes remained popular, and there was a vogue for thimbles bearing their owner's initials. The Rhode Island Historical Society possesses three mid-seventeenth-century thimbles, one of which is a sewing ring bearing an engraved heart and inscribed 'Esther Willit – 1660–1665'. The earliest commemorative thimble, celebrating the marriage of Charles II to Katherine of Braganza in 1662, which can be seen in the Museum of London, is an equally fascinating contemporary piece.

A Sewing Compendium

A 17th-century ivory sewing compendium, probably French. The ivory has been pierced with decorative punches in an identical manner to the thimbles of the time. The thimble unscrews from its base which would have held bodkins and needles. The figure on the front of the compendium sports a headdress typical of the French court. The compendium recently reached £400 at sale.

EIGHTEENTH-CENTURY THIMBLES

Three main shapes characterize thimbles made

in the eighteenth century: in the early years, a

short, round thimble was preferred; gradually,

tall, thin thimbles replaced these in popularity;

but by the end of the century, the beehive form

was favoured. As the century progressed, so the

demand for sewing sets increased.

By the end of the seventeenth century, the Dutch thimble industry was beginning to lose its business to English and German competitors. There were at least five German factories in the valley of the river Lenne, in south Westphalia, the most notable of which was owned by Johan Casper Rumpe who enjoyed the patronage of Frederick the Great. Rumpe's basic method of production was casting and then hand-finishing and his company specialized in inexpensive well-made metal thimbles; they are still in production today.

England had its own prospering brass trade by now and no longer needed to import thimbles from overseas. John Lofting's mill continued production into the eighteenth century—finds of his brass thimbles in the United States, England and the Netherlands suggest that they were in great demand. Birmingham had a flourishing trade in small brass toys (in the sense of trinkets), such as thimbles, buckles and buttons, alongside that of its silverware. Joseph Ashwell and Walter Davenport were registered there in the trade directory in 1769 as thimble-makers. The same year saw the patenting of an important invention for applying metal ornamentation, John Ford's patent Number 935. Raised patterns were formed on a sheet of metal which was pressed by machine between two dyes (stamps), one dye being convex and the other concave. This gave far greater scope for design on

Above: *A pair of mid 18th-century gold 'Freedom' thimbles. The thimbles are inscribed 'The Freedom of the Corporation of Tailors, Ambe, leet, Master, 1768'. £5500, Sotheby's London 1984. One of the reasons they fetched such a high price is that their provenance is well-documented.*

less expensive goods and effectively foreshadowed the end of the hand-crafted metal thimble; after a period of experimentation, mass-production of metal thimbles became a reality.

The collector's interest in base metal thimbles is obviously not connected solely with the value of the materials from which they are made or with aesthetic considerations, but with their craftsmanship, antiquity, historical associations and so on. The mass-production of thimbles therefore often renders them less interesting to the collector.

Two Sewing Compendiums

Two 18th-century European silver sewing compendiums. In each the thimble unscrews from its base which would have held needles and cotton thread on a reel. The bases of such compendiums were often used to stamp sealing wax on letters. Each of them is decorated, the one with a trailing ribbon design popular in the Renaissance, the other with a Moorish pattern. These were sold recently for £650 each.

The eighteenth century saw the general diminution of the power of monarchy and a corresponding increase in the power of elected government. New industrial methods accelerated the number and range of everyday and luxury goods produced and more people could afford them. The eighteenth-century fashion for trifles, *objets de vertu*, and *galenterie* (including thimbles) which originated in France, took Europe by storm. Silver sewing compendiums are a good example.

Three main thimble shapes succeeded each other as the century progressed. Needleworkers in the first half of the century preferred the shorter rounder shape which then declined in popularity in favour of a return to the tall, slim thimble with a rounded top. The beehive form towards the end of the century was the last of the three. Until the 1750s or so, thimbles were still being made in two pieces—a top and a cylinder. A gentle widening of the base in relation to the top as the century progressed was accompanied by the addition of a border which often carried decoration, followed by two engraved lines at the thimble's base (in lieu of a rim). Indentations were small and round, retaining the circular look prevalent at the

EIGHTEENTH-CENTURY THIMBLES

Right: *An 18th-century European gold thimble. The combination of the hand punches and the engraved design give the thimble a rather hand-made appearance. It was valued in 1989 at £350.*

Above: *Two late 18th-century gold thimbles with steel tops. The smaller thimble was made for a child.*

end of the previous century—the waffle indentations on the sides of the thimbles had ceased. Occasionally tiny dots were used in between the circular indentations. The thimble tops had both round and waffle-shaped indentations but rarely any rims.

In the second half of the century, metal thimbles began to be made in one piece using a technique known as the 'deep drawn' method. 'Deep drawing' shapes the thimble from a small, flat, round disc which is hammered into a dye, or mould. This method of production was largely responsible for pushing the trend towards taller slimmer thimbles which needed in some cases to be reinforced, for instance, with the introduction of steel tops. Beehive thimbles were made in one piece, with indentations reaching down to the border at their base. Thimble decoration certainly changed to suit current tastes (for the Neo-classical and Rococo styles), but not so drastically that working thimbles lost their primarily functional raison d'être. The more restrained Neo-classical style prevailed on decorative thimbles that had still to retain their full function; more extravagant Rococo designs were favoured for elaborate chatelaines and etuis, prized for their fine workmanship and expensive materials more than for their utility. Exceptional workmanship is evident in certain Rococo gold and tortoiseshell thimble cases and in gold thimbles. The typically wavy, almost waisted outline, the chasing of tiny flowers and leaves and even the use of a natural material such as shell in luxurious harmony with gold are all classic examples of the Rococo style at its finest.

THIMBLES AS TOYS

Decorative thimbles and other 'toys' were also being introduced alongside practical working thimbles. Silver compendiums, mainly made in England, Germany and Italy are particularly interesting: a compendium unscrews to reveal a thimble, a letter powderer, a needle-holder and a letter seal. Ribbon-like interlacing and chasing in Moorish patterns recurs frequently. Filigree (wire work) was widely applied to sewing toys, and in the first half of the century, decorative filigree

Left: *A mid to late 18th-century European silver thimble. The punches are now very mechanical in appearance.*

Above: *A late 18th-century gold thimble with its gold and tortoiseshell case in the Rococo style. The case is beautifully chased with leaf and flower motifs. £2600, 1989.*

Above and above right:
A mid 18th-century Meissen porcelain thimble. These four views of the same thimble allow the movement and 'action' of the figures portrayed to be followed around the whole thimble, fully illustrating the famous charm and quality of Meissen's hand painting.

Right above and below: *Three scenes from a single mid 18th-century Meissen porcelain thimble. The three panels contain exquisitely detailed and delicate seascapes and landscapes.*

letters. Most of the toys that have survived are in silver, gold or pinchbeck and command very high prices. Contemporary porcelain thimbles are also highly sought-after: the vital factor affecting their value is the painting on them. They have the added charm of often being very colourful, with an air of fragile delicacy.

The eighteenth century was the great age of porcelain, a fine ceramic ware, white, translucent and very delicate. It was first developed and exploited in China and was named after its country of origin, although the English word comes from the Italian, *porcellana*.

Unfortunately very few porcelain thimbles of the period exist, and many of those that have come down to us are difficult to attribute with any certainty. Because of this, accredited eighteenth-century porcelain thimbles are highly sought-after and consequently fetch very high prices at auction.

MEISSEN

One of the first documented porcelain thimbles is recorded in the list of the great Meissen factory (the first to manufacture 'hard paste' porcelain in Europe) in Germany in the early 1700s, under the category *Galanterien,* which can be translated in this context as 'fancy goods'. There is little pretence that these porcelain thimbles were ever intended for practical work: they were fashioned purely as decorative objects—as beautiful gifts and keepsakes for wives and sweethearts—and for this reason they have a very special place in the romance of thimble-collecting (China thimbles do, however, have a specific use in needlework, as their smooth texture makes them ideal for working with silk).

Because most Meissen thimbles now exist in private collections, it is very difficult to calculate how many actually survive, but it would be a great surprise, given what we know, if there are more than about 500—of which only a handful are in public collections and museums. At probably the most important ever auction of thimbles, held at Christie's Geneva showroom in 1975, no less than 103 Meissen thimbles went under the hammer, all of which were fully authenti-

thimbles were stubby in shape and had rounded tops. Later filigrees are taller and slimmer, but both styles had shields or ovals on which their owner's initials could be marked.

Various combinations were used in making later thimble toys, the most famous being a thimble screwing on to a base containing a miniature scent bottle as first seen in the preceding century. Other variations included thimbles with a tape measure or a pin cushion. Some had a finger guard that screwed on to a base containing a tiny emery cushion; the guard was then covered by a thimble, but is sadly, now almost always missing. The bases of these toys often had engraved initials and are thought to have been used to seal

Left: *Three views of a single Meissen thimble showing the message 'Je Y Pense', underneath a delightful rustic panorama.*

cated, and many of which were, in addition, accredited to individual craftsmen and painters. A world record price of 21,000 Swiss francs was paid for a continuous seascape thimble featuring offshore ships, attributed to Ignaz Preissler at Breslau. This record price was broken in 1979, when Christie's auctioned 10 Meissen thimbles, among them a small thimble from the 1740s depicting a harbour scene, which sold for a hammer price of £8000.

Landscapes and seascapes are popular Meissen subjects, as are people fishing or hunting, and birds and flowers depicted in oriental style. Many Meissen thimbles have a distinctive rounded form, but the Cummer Gallery of Art in Jacksonville, Florida, has a collection of eight eighteenth-century Meissen thimbles, the shapes of which vary considerably. One has a waisted effect, tied around with a painted blue bow on a plain white ground and with a gilded interior; another is very small and squat, with two plain yellow bands at top and bottom; and a third has a flat top, is tall and slim, and is painted all over with many-coloured 'Deutsche-Blumen' flowers. This Deutsche-Blumen pattern was introduced *c.*1735, inspired by Chinese and Japanese work: it shows stylized oriental flowers outlined in a darker colour.

The trademark of Meissen consists of two crossed swords, painted in underglaze blue, but this is not always present. Meissen thimbles can usually be readily identified by the painting style, which is always fine, and shows meticulous attention to detail: gilding inside

the thimble is also a good indicator, but again, this is not always found.

Meissen designs were heavily influenced by Chinese and Japanese decoration on the costly items regularly imported to Europe from the Far East at that time. Because of their great commercial success, and the facility with which they reinterpreted oriental hard paste porcelain, most of their contemporary European rivals copied Meissen, though there is not here, as there is in other thimble categories, much danger of confusion in attribution. These competitors and imitators included factories at Furstenberg, Ludwigburg, Nymphenburg, and possibly Höchst, in Germany; Schooren in Switzerland; and Du Paquier in Vienna: but documentation is incomplete, and in any case none of their production can be said to rival Meissen either in artistry or scale of output.

Elsewhere in Europe, the Royal Copenhagen factory in Denmark certainly produced some porcelain thimbles, but they lack the refined elegance of their Meissen peers. Thimbles were also manufactured at the Royal Factory in Naples, Italy, of which a small number still exist, and at Mennecy-Villeroy, in France. However, it is only in England that any genuine attempt was made to compete with Meissen, certainly in quantity, if seldom in design. It is ironic that the growth of the market for porcelain thimbles in England came at a time when the Meissen factory had all but ceased production.

Generally, records for the earliest part of the

Left: *Three views of a single Meissen thimble, c.1740, show a highly typical hunting scene of a man out shooting, with his dog retrieving a fallen bird. The thimble has red cross hatching over its top which seems to have been worn away by use.*

Right: *A Meissen porcelain thimble, c.1760. It has a gilded rim, and a pretty garland of orange, blue and pink flowers around its base.*

Above: *A late 18th-century English porcelain thimble. Two views of a Chelsea soft paste thimble with 'Pour ce que j'aime' ('For the one I love') written around it: one side shows a red-crested bird with bright plumage sitting in foliage, and the other depicts a bird in flight.*

eighteenth century are vague, and though thimbles other than Meissen have come down to us, attribution is difficult and mostly uncertain. Factory documentation shows that porcelain thimbles were being manufactured in quantity, yet relatively few examples exist: this may be due to their fragility, or to the fact that they were damaged easily, and so were discarded.

In England in the late eighteenth century, the Chelsea factory and the Worcester Porcelain Company (previously named Chamberlain Worcester), all included soft paste thimbles in their list of wares. It was not until the nineteenth century that the fashion really took hold, and the market was then quickly dominated by Worcester.

Porcelain had become a standard product by the end of the eighteenth century: when Chamberlain (later to become Chamberlain Worcester) commenced manufacture in 1790, there were fewer than 10 porcelain producers in the British Isles, but by the 1840s–50s there were nearly 100. One of the earliest pieces of evidence of porcelain thimble manufacture in England is a thimble waster, or mould, found in one of the store rooms of the Worcester Porcelain Company dating from c.1785. The 1795 Christmas stocktaking at Chamberlain recorded 300 unglazed thimbles for sale at one penny each, and an order page dated January 1 1796 shows a stock of 25 dozen Worcester thimbles, with a further 66 in the Chamberlain shop, proving that significant thimble production existed at that time. There is some evidence of a limited production of Derby porcelain thimbles; in the list of moulds, one entry in 1795 refers to 'eight thimbles'.

Many of the soft paste thimbles produced by the Chelsea factory bear French mottoes such as, for instance, 'Gage de mon amitié', which is found on one example in the Victoria and Albert Museum. Since the fashion for toy thimbles came from France, British manufacturers would regularly add French inscriptions to their pieces.

Right: *One early and two late 18th-century English silver thimbles, the early thimble inscribed 'IF'.*

Right: *Two 18th-century English steel-topped silver thimbles, made by the silversmith Hester Bateman, both bearing the initials 'HB'.*

Left: *An 18th-century steel-topped silver thimble with a delightful novelty rim. It was probably made for a child and is decorated with a tea caddy, a squirrel, teacups and a teapot, and a pair of sugar tongs or scissors.*

The more expensive English thimbles of this period were not made exclusively of porcelain however: aside from purely functional, practical thimbles in base metals, very fine examples continued to be made in silver. One of the earliest silversmiths whom it is possible to name is Hester Bateman, a fine craftswoman, who lived in London, producing objects between 1761–1790, including excellent working thimbles in a controlled Neo-classical style. If the border of a Bateman thimble is closely examined, the initials 'HB' will be found chased into the pattern, rather than stamped on with the customary silver punch: this may have been a means of avoiding assay office costs on these small items. Many Hester Bateman thimbles are steel-topped.

London was not the only place in England producing high-quality silverware. The rise of Birmingham as a manufacturing city producing silver objects of significance first became evident in the latter half of the seventeenth century, and its position was finally assured when Matthew Bolton, a silversmith and businessman, managed to obtain permission to open an assay office there in 1773. Before this, all goods had to be sent to London for taxing, which could often result in delay, and sometimes in theft and damage. Important manufacturers such as Matthew Linwood, Matthew Arnold, and Samuel Pemberton all founded substantial silver-working companies in the area, each of which maintained a large output of thimbles.

The eighteenth-century also saw the serious development of thimbles in enamel. The word is derived from the French *amail* or *esmail* and enamel itself is made from a mixture of silica, minium and potash, which when it is in its molten state, is coloured with various chemicals and then fused on to a metallic surface. Some enamel is transparent and some opaque. The decoration thus achieved is particularly fragile—more so even than porcelain—and it is very rare to find genuine antique enamel thimbles in good condition. It is probably this delicacy which has prevented more thimbles from coming down to us from earlier periods. Most enamel thimbles are made on a base of silver, copper or steel, with the sides left free for elaborate decorative painting.

Enamel thimbles were never widely produced, and classic enamel thimble manufacture was limited principally to the eighteenth and nineteenth centuries, primarily in England. Foremost among the enamel thimble producers were factories at Bilston and south Staffordshire, in the English Midlands.

In the United States, there is very little evidence of early porcelain thimble manufacture, and although there was a limited production of silver and base metal thimbles, almost all of the silver thimbles used until the eighteenth century were imported. Three generations of craftsmen, the Richardsons, are known to have worked in Philadelphia from 1681 onwards into the eighteenth century, and there are records of Joseph Richardson, silversmith, topping silver

Above: *An 18th-century ormolu chatelaine. Valued at £530 in 1989.*

Above: *An 18th-century ormolu chatelaine in the Rococo style. Valued at £600 in 1989.*

thimbles with steel. Although English silversmiths concentrated on making the newly-fashionable tall, slim thimbles as the century progressed, American craftsmen retained their preference for a shorter, stubbier style: indeed, American thimbles look noticeably shorter than European thimbles throughout the eighteenth, nineteenth and early twentieth centuries.

Although these records exist of the early producers, it is not until the 1760s that there is evidence of anyone claiming to specialize solely in thimble manufacture. Probably the first American to promote himself exclusively as a thimble-maker was one Benjamin Halstead, of New York and Philadelphia—in fact he was confident enough to advertise in 1794 that his production was now large enough to supply the whole United States, and that citizens should therefore boycott lower-quality imported thimbles. His business flourished—though his claims about the superiority of his product to the imported thimbles were highly tenuous—and there is evidence that his son opened a separate manufacturing unit on Varick Street, New York, c.1814.

Pinchbeck Thimbles
Many eighteenth-century thimbles were made of a copper and zinc alloy called 'Pinchbeck', although the name is often loosely applied to objects of similar composition from the following century (though purists use the term only to apply to articles actually made by Christopher Pinchbeck, a London clock- and watchmaker who worked in the first half of the eighteenth century). Good-quality Pinchbeck was often gilded, did not tarnish and was virtually indistinguishable from real gold, but later and less expensive Victorian Pinchbeck pieces are duller and closely resemble brass. Continental companies also produced jewellery in imitations of Pinchbeck that resembled gold, which sometimes went by the name 'Similor' or 'goldshine'.

ENAMEL THIMBLES

Most enamel thimbles have the decoration

applied to a base of silver or copper, with

indentations on the top only and the sides left

free for the elaborate decorative devices. The

thimbles were never intended for working use,

and this meant that designs could be of the most

delicate beauty.

Enamelling is a decorative art which involves the covering of a metal surface with special types of glass in their molten or liquid form (more properly described as vitreous) and then firing the object to give a hard, glazed finish. The decoration thus achieved is particularly fragile – more so, even, than porcelain – and it is very rare to find genuinely antique enamel thimbles in good condition. It is probably this delicacy which has prevented more thimbles from coming down to us from earlier periods.

Enamel thimbles were never very widely produced, and classic enamel thimble manufacture was limited principally to the eighteenth and nineteenth centuries, mainly in England. It possibly gained favour during those periods because enamel craftsmen saw it as a way to profit by copying the very successful porcelain designs of Meissen and their other European imitators – certainly the style and patterns are very similar. Foremost among the enamel thimble producers were factories at Bilston and South Staffordshire, in the English Midlands, and Battersea, in London: their work was in turn copied by some minor factories in Germany and France. Enamel thimble production still continues today in Norway and Germany, to a highly reduced degree; the thimbles are really manufactured only as side-lines by specialist enamelling factories.

Above: *An attractive group of enamel thimbles. The three on the right are south Staffordshire, 19th century, featuring flower* designs. *The attribution of the thimble on the extreme left is less certain, but it is possibly 19th-century Persian.*

ENAMEL COPIES

Antique enamel thimbles are so scarce today that it is a lucky collector indeed who has one. So perhaps of more interest to most collectors is the existence of a wide range of imitations.

The south Staffordshire factories were very successful, and as always in the world of thimbles, there were other companies keen to snatch some of this success for themselves. The moment one factory did very

Right: *An English enamel thimble, south Staffordshire, late 18th- or early 19th-century, depicting ladies promenading in cloaks. Enamel of this period is often difficult to date accurately.*

Right: *A late 19th-century enamel thimble with a hole in its top. The hole may have been made by the mould during the production process, or, less likely, this may have been designed as a peep.*

Right: *A late 19th-century or early 20th-century enamel thimble with a rather unusual shape, featuring an impressionistic representation of brightly coloured flowers.*

Above: *Russian cloisonné work, including thimbles, have also been copied very closely. The thimble on the left is original; on the right is a fake Russian thimble of enamel on silver gilt, which even has the '84' stamp illicitly reproduced on the rim to add authenticity. The thimble is much heavier and thicker than the original because it has been cast from an old mould; the enamel is also cruder and brighter. Value: at 1990 prices, the fake would fetch £30 and the original, subject to its condition and provenance, £1550.*

well with a product, other factories would pirate their designs and, in some cases, any identifying marks. This practice continued into the nineteenth and twentieth centuries. The imitators were not attempting to fake antiques, but rather to copy successful designs. The distinction between fakes and copies is not always very clear, however, and the subject of enamel thimbles is a controversial one in various ways.

Samson and Company, founded in Paris in 1845, was just one of the many companies that copied eighteenth-century enamel designs, both as straightforward copies bearing their own Samson mark and as fakes ie exact copies of the original eighteenth-century pieces, sometimes with their original marks. A comparison of an eighteenth-century original and a later Samson copy will reveal that the brushwork on the original is freer and more fluent, that the enamel has more life and sheen, and that the colours on the thimble are not so powdery. As a general rule, the art of copying forces any artist into stiffness in reproducing detail accurately. Samson, among various companies in Europe also producing copies, issued their first replicas of eighteenth-century enamel thimbles *c.*1850. Copies of porcelain and enamel eighteenth-century bibelots were also popular with the Victorian middle classes, following the 1862 Special Exhibition of Works at the South Kensington Museum (now the Victoria and Albert Museum). Many replicas were made and indeed up until 1930,

Lady Charlotte and Charles Schreiber

Lady Charlotte and Charles Schreiber MP. Lady Charlotte donated her collection of 18th- and 19th-century enamel and porcelain wares and sewing compendiums to the Victoria and Albert Museum. The enamel thimbles in the collection are the most important ever assembled. These portraits are made of mosaic and are framed in wood.

the Samson showrooms in Paris had rooms allotted to replicas of different periods.

Emile Samson was an acute businessman and appreciated that his customers did not always want their copies marked as Samson pieces, as they wished to show them off as eighteenth-century originals. Some pieces carried the crossed 'S' for Samson, others did not (or the mark was removed by their later owners). Samson also sometimes reproduced and applied marks such as Meissen's crossed swords or Chelsea's red anchor if requested to do so by a purchaser.

Nineteenth- and twentieth-century copies of eighteenth-century thimble holders lack the fine metal mounts or hinges and have a central metal 'lug' (useful for identification on some thimble cases and egg-shaped étuis) to stop the lid opening too far. The mounts on the copies were often machined in a notched pattern to their outer edge. Samson and Company rarely used transfer prints on copies (unlike other European copiers) such was their pride in their freehand painting.

Samson copies continued to be made until they became too expensive for the customer; in 1975, a London antique dealer purchased the company's enamelling machinery. There is no documentary

Left: *An interesting little metal thimble—possibly Greek or Russian— decorated with a disproportionately large Cyrillic letter in red enamel.*

Above: *A beautiful group of modern Norwegian enamel thimbles. These are a reissue by David Andersen of the famous Norwegian enamel on gilded silver thimbles originally made at the beginning of the 20th century.* **(Left to Right)** *A viking ship; the midnight sun; a polar bear; and reindeer. The reissues differ from the antiques in having a waffle top rather than a moonstone top.*

evidence to suggest that Samson definitely copied eighteenth-century thimble designs. The only evidence is hearsay and the comparison of Samson pieces with earlier enamel objects. Shape alone is not conclusive proof of authentic or copied items, and metal-testing of the metal under the enamel is both inaccurate and unhelpful as there are insufficient data with which to compare the results.

In my opinion only an understanding of enamel painting, its application and the colours used combined with a feeling for the period can give you enough confidence to date an object.

Above: *Four 20th-century enamel thimbles.* **(Left to Right)** *A commemorative celebrating Queen Elizabeth's Silver Jubilee; a German thimble made for the Dutch market—enamel on silver; then another Jubilee commemorative; and a stylish modern Norwegian enamel.*

Left: *A group of charming modern inexpensive Austrian enamel thimbles made as souvenirs for tourists who want a memento of their travels.*

NINETEENTH-CENTURY THIMBLES

In the early years of the century, the sphinx was

a popular motif used in Neo-classical designs.

By the 1830s, however, designs had become

much more naturalistic, and examples of this

style co-existed with those of the great Gothic

revival. Decoration made after 1870 often

reflected the oriental interests of the

Aesthetic movement.

The nineteenth century was without doubt the golden age of thimble design and manufacture. In general, the first forty or so years of the century—roughly encompassing the French Empire and English Regency periods—were marked by a mood of cautious optimism, unlike the more carefree and comfortable decades that followed. This early watchful yet discerning temperament was reflected in the abundance of delightful, sometimes even frivolous—but rarely highly precious, as in the previous century—*objets de vertu*, including thimbles. High-quality but relatively affordable thimbles and sewing items, such as the mother-of-pearl Palais Royal type from Paris, were being produced on the one hand, while on the other, bone, Prisoner of War work, scrimshaw and Tonbridge ware were made as less expensive novelties. Strawwork, pen work and scrolled-paper examples were

made, largely out of necessity and in the face of abject poverty throughout much of Europe.

By the middle of the century, however, times were getting better: the debilitating effects of the Napoleonic wars were diminishing and the overall European economy was improving. Concomitantly, the manufacture and popular use of thimbles made of precious metals increased, with silver, and two- and three-coloured gold varieties especially favoured, the latter often in sharkskin (also called shagreen, or *galuchat*) cases. Brass and base-metal thimbles continued to be made in the 1800s, these generally mass-produced in huge quantities, and were of good quality considering their competitive price. The main producers were based in Germany in south Westphalia, and in and around Birmingham in England.

The development of the primarily nineteenth-century phenomenon, the international trade fair,

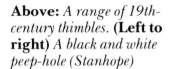

Above: *A range of 19th-century thimbles.* **(Left to right)** *A black and white peep-hole (Stanhope)* *thimble; a 19th-century Worcester porcelain thimble with a cream ground, gilt bands at the* *top and bottom and blue and pink droplets; a silver filigree thimble, c.1840; a* *gold thimble decorated with garnets.*

resulted in the display of thimbles from all over the globe, particularly European examples. These huge exhibitions were held regularly throughout the years in many locations, a significant proportion of them in France, but others in Great Britain, the United States, Australia and elsewhere. Local craftsmen would have been exposed to, and no doubt inspired by, the fine works on display at these fairs, thimbles among them. As a result, general standards of design and manufacture tended to rise, and even goods at the lowest end of the price scale, made of the most common materials —and by means of mass-production—could be appealing and well-crafted.

GENERAL DESIGN AND CONSTRUCTION
For about the first two decades of the century, the most common thimbles were domed like a beehive, their sides slightly wider than their tops, with fine indentations often reaching down the sides to meet decorative borders. One-part thimble construction was favoured for silver and gold versions. From around 1830 thimbles grew slightly taller and lost their bee-hive shape. Finger-guards became very popular as well, and these were often offered in a set with a matching thimble. Some of the most refined sewing sets ever made date from this period, such as those in mother-of-pearl from the Palais Royal area of Paris.

Factory production increased markedly by the middle of the century, accelerating the decline of the hand-made object and making many talented craftsmen jobless. In Britain especially the rise of industry (including improved rail transportation) engendered the age of the mass-manufactured object including thimbles for general use. In general, from the middle of the century thimbles grew even taller and more decorative, retaining their slim shapes and rounded tops. The base-metal thimble took yet another blow, however, with the invention of the sewing machine: the industrial revolution, introducing affordable, mass-produced clothing for the first time, combined with the new facility for clothes to be machine-made at home, meant that eventually the demand for the humble working thimble (though not for its glamorous, ornate counterpart) was to plummet dramatically.

'Prisoner of War work' was produced in the European period of extreme poverty often known as the Hungry '40s. There were thimbles, thimble cases and finger-guards of bone, naively decorated with black and red hearts, others with anchors.

To the list of thimbles made from unusual or rare materials must be added amber examples, amber being a yellowish, translucent fossil resin found mainly on the southern Baltic coast. Amber thimbles were usually mounted in gold or silver; some were hallmarked on the rim, and yet others were sold in an amber hussif or needlecase.

NINETEENTH-CENTURY THIMBLES

SCOTTISH WARES

Sewing tools such as needle holders, pincushions, shuttles and thimbles, as well as snuff boxes and various desk accessories, were made of three types of Scottish wares: Mauchline ware, Fern ware and Tartan ware.

The Mauchline ware industry was started by two brothers, William and Andrew Smith, of Mauchline, Ayrshire, Scotland. From the early 1820s they produced these delightful wooden wares, the earliest examples bearing painted and varnished scenes of famous local beauty spots. The direct application of paint on wood was replaced in the 1840s by scenes that were painted onto square or oval pieces of paper, glued to the wood and then varnished. Subsequent items were produced by direct transfer-printing and later (c.1890) even monochrome prints were applied. Although most Mauchline ware, which was primarily intended for the tourist trade, was decorated with Scottish and English scenes, occasional export pieces with American, Continental or even exotic Indian or other colonial scenes were made.

Fern ware, dating from around the 1880s, was decorated with either ferns or ferns and shells. Early varieties tend to resemble fossil prints.

Below: *Among the most popular Victorian thimbles was the famous English 'Piercy's patent thimble', which was made of tortoiseshell combined with gold, silver or a mixture of both metals. Such thimbles have a precious-metal indented top, a tortoiseshell body and a shield flanked by a lion and a unicorn, with the words 'Piercy's patent' inscribed underneath. Variations on this design occur, such as the shield-bearing version assuming an off-centre or crooked look: this is typical, and not a mistake. The patent was registered c.1816.*

Right: *A range of Tartan-ware in excellent condition, including emery (McDuff tartan); tape measure (McLean); stamp holder (Albert); thimble holder (Stuart); and pen wiper (Stuart).*

Right: *A fine collection of fern ware, c.1886–90.* (**Left to Right**) *A thimble holder; a shamrock shaped pin cushion; a pin tray* (**behind**)*; a pin cushion; and a needle book.*

40

Arguably the most popular of these Scottish pieces were those of Tartan ware, wherein tartan-decorated paper was carefully applied to wood surfaces and then varnished. Earlier pieces were painted, and some even included landscapes set in tartan medallions. Later, such images were replaced by prints and photographs, sometimes of an important person or place within a tartan border.

TUNBRIDGE WARE THIMBLES

Tunbridge ware thimbles appeared in the early 1800s. Of simple turned wood such as yew or holly, these charming thimbles—which were originally tourist gifts made in Tunbridge Wells, Kent, a town whose well water was renowned for its curative powers—were often painted with delicate bands of red, green and yellow. Tunbridge ware usually took the form of boxes and games, with various sewing implements also produced. The later variety of Tunbridge ware known as 'stick ware' was also employed for thimbles, but such examples are extremely rare, as they were highly impractical to use (being made of small slivers of vari-coloured woods pressed together and coated with adhesive). On the whole, in fact, wood is not a good material for thimbles, since its softness makes it prone to split.

Above: *A mid 19th-century silver thimble with a 'cable' or scalloped edge. Note the taller, slimmer shape, and the applied decorative border. This example has no hallmark. That the thimble played a significant role in nineteenth-century communications technology is a fact little known to the general public. But most thimble collectors will know that a humble thimble was once used as a battery in order to send a message through the Atlantic telegraph cable from Valentia Island, Ireland, to White Sand Bay in Newfoundland. The notable 'Atlantic Cable Thimble', as it is known today, belonged to Miss Emily Fitzgerald, daughter of the Knight of Kerry, and it is now in the Science Museum in London.*

Above: *Three fine examples of 19th-century Tunbridge thimbles. The one on the right is a piece of stickware and, valued at over £500 ($800), is one of the most expensive pieces of wood in the world.*

Left: *Early 19th-century painted and inlaid Tunbridge ware c.1820. The black thimble in the middle is made of bog oak, and the thimble egg in the upper left-hand corner is inlaid stick ware.*

GOLD THIMBLES

Gold thimbles are not in the main hallmarked, so it is not very simple to ascertain the gold content, ie, their carat. In general, however, Victorian thimbles were made in 15-carat gold, with 9-carat examples appearing in the late nineteenth century and made through to the beginning of the twentieth. The basic guideline to follow is that the heavier the gold, the higher the carat (though there are always exceptions).

In the nineteenth century, France and Switzerland generally used 18-carat gold (lower carats were not recognized as gold there), Great Britain used 9-, 15- and 18-carat gold, and the United States preferred 14- and occasionally 18-carat gold. German gold is accepted as low as 8 carats, but such pieces are more often of twentieth-century vintage.

Left: *A 19th-century gold thimble with a very elegant border.*

Right: (Left to Right) *An unusual coral top which fetched £300 in 1989; and three gold 19th-century thimbles which sold, also in 1989, for £250 each.*

Right: *A handsome group of 19th-century gold and gem-set thimbles, showing a stunning range of sizes, designs, and ornamentation.*

Left: (Left to Right) *A fine English gold thimble decorated with a grape device more often seen on American examples; a highly decorated thimble, including a very attractive border of pearls and turquoise; and an English thimble, c.1850–60, with a beautiful design consisting of a flower with a long stamen coming out of the middle and a deep border.*

Right: *19th-century enamel gold and stone-set thimbles, including two with pearls, two with turquoise, and one decorated with raised grapes. The pale blue enamel band was a popular Victorian design.*

Amazingly, there are 48 registered colours of gold (although you cannot discern the carat of gold by its colour). The most common varieties are white gold (gold mixed with silver), rose gold (gold mixed with copper), green gold (gold mixed with various alloys) and pure gold, which is of the 24-carat variety but is somewhat rare due to its impractical soft state.

If a piece of gold does not have a hallmark (that is, carat mark), a professional jeweller can use the so-called acid test to ascertain exactly what the carat of the gold is or whether the article is merely gold-plated.

Instead of a hallmark, so-called convention marks often appear: 18-carat gold is marked '750', 14-carat is '585' and 9-carat is '375', and on imported goods, 22-carat gold is stamped '916', 18-carat '750', 14-carat '585' and 9-carat '375'. Over the years, British gold standards have been lowered: up to 1798, 22-carat was the standard; from 1798 to 1854, 22- and 18-carat; from 1854 to 1931, 9-, 12- and 15-carat, and since 1931, 9-, 12- and 14-carat.

Above: *Gold gem-set thimbles on which the gems spell out 'Regard': 'R' from ruby, 'E' from emerald, 'G' from garnet, 'A' from amethyst, 'R' from ruby and 'D' from diamond.*

GEM-SET THIMBLES

Many gold thimbles are set with real gemstones, which are generally colder to the touch than simulated stones made from porcelain, enamel, glass or early plastic. Some dealers test the authenticity of gemstones by biting them—they are supposed to be harder. I do not recommend this—it can cause dental problems. More crucial to the thimble collector than whether a stone is genuine or not, is whether it is original to its setting. A replacement stone, even if it is intrinsically valuable, takes away from the authenticity of a piece, thus lowering its quality and its value to the collector.

Victorian thimbles often contained so-called 'jewels', which were in fact drops of porcelain or coloured enamel (these usually reminiscent of coral or turquoise) or bits of glass (resembling amethysts, garnets and the like). Interestingly enough, real turquoise is porous and prone to discolouration, so the pretty, evenly coloured blue stones imitating the gemstone are often thought of as the real thing, and the actual, often discoloured stone is falsely assumed to be the fake. Semi-precious agate and cornelian were often used instead of glass in stone top thimbles, particularly since they were then nearly as cheap as glass.

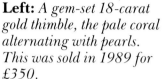

Left: *A gem-set 18-carat gold thimble, the pale coral alternating with pearls. This was sold in 1989 for £350.*

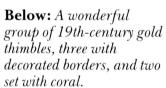

Below: *A wonderful group of 19th-century gold thimbles, three with decorated borders, and two set with coral.*

Right: *Two gold gem-set thimbles, one (left) with garnets and the other (right) with amethysts. Valued in 1990 at £350 each.*

Above: *An extremely fine, and rather rare 19th-century 18-carat gold thimble, probably c.1870, set with diamonds and sapphires. With it is its case – an octagonal box with alternating mother-of-pearl panels in white and a golden shade formed by cleverly leaving in the outer 'skin' of the mother-of-pearl which is normally carved away. The set was valued in 1989 at £780.*

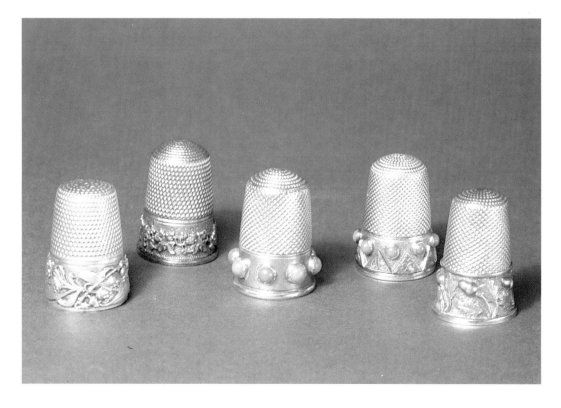

Left: *An interesting group of enamel and gold 19th-century thimbles with striking graphic designs. The thimble on the right is set with pearls.*

Left: *A 19th-century gold thimble set with turquoise, which was valued in 1989 at £250.*

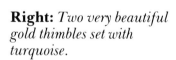

Right: *Two very beautiful gold thimbles set with turquoise.*

Above: *A mid 19th-century gold thimble, slightly beehive-shaped, with pretty forget-me-nots finely set all around the rim, the flowers picked out in stones. Valued in 1989 at £450.*

CHATELAINES, ETUIS AND OTHER SEWING ACCESSORIES

Châtelaines, étuis, nécessaires, sewing boxes and various other containers or accessories can greatly enhance a thimble collection. A châtelaine, which hung from a clasp or hook suspended from the waist, comprised several chains supporting separate items such as a thimble in a case, scissors or a notebook and pen. An étui, on the other hand, is a single container in which a variety of items is held; it can be portable, for carrying in a pocket, or simply kept on a table, like a smaller sewing box. Etui cases are often elaborately decorated and can be of gold or pinchbeck mounted with, for example, tortoiseshell and malachite or mother-of-pearl. Nécessaire is a general term covering any small container, including a sewing box. In the

Above and left: *A 19th-century sewing set. The box is damascened – inlaid with metal in an Arabic style – and the tools themselves are steel.*

Below: *A 19th-century ivory French sewing set (c.1870), with silver gilt fittings, sold for £390 in 1989.*

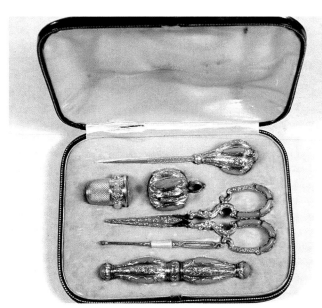

Above: *A 19th-century boxed set in a leather case. The tools are silver gilt with coral, and consist of a stiletto tape measure, a thimble, scissors, a bodkin and a needlecase.*

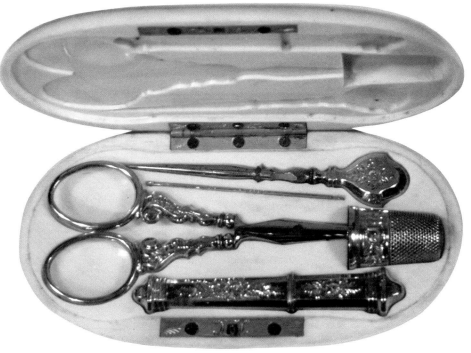

1880s the leather-boxed sewing set, or nécessaire, was extremely popular throughout Europe; an English example from the time comprises a leather case with a silver-gilt sewing set inlaid with corals.

Chatelaines have the longest ancestry of these accessories: their history can be traced back to Norman times. Over the years they fell in and out of fashion. A man's version, the 'Macaroni', was particularly popular with eighteenth-century dandies, and was commonly worn in pairs, on either side, attached to the belt. A wide variety of chatelaines were in great demand throughout the nineteenth century, from the Romantic period of the 1810s (when medieval and Renaissance revival designs of gold, pinchbeck, cut steel and silver were made), to the time of the Great Exhibition of 1851 (where these 'amusing little trifles' were noted with wry amusement by a writer in the *Illustrated London News*) to the 1890s, when cut-steel and silver versions proliferated.

Boxed sewing sets were made not only in Europe, but also in the East, as evidenced by an unusual 18-carat gold Indian set of the nineteenth century, almost certainly made by the Pertabgarh workshops in Rasputana, northern India. Beautiful enamelled plaques fashioned by local craftsmen sometimes adorn the boxes which enclose a thimble, Indian or otherwise, and scissors.

Left: *Three gold thimbles.* (**Left to Right**) *19th-century, gold with blue enamel; c.1800, plain gold; and 19th-century gold set with turquoise.*

Above: *A 19th-century French sewing set in a handsome oval leather box. The tools are of gold set with blue enamel.*

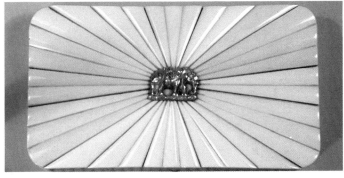

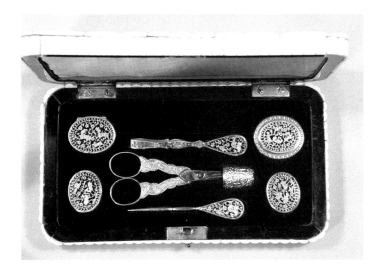

Left and above: *An open and closed box showing an Indian elephant on the front. The tools are very fine and ornate, and the set was valued at £2800 in 1990.*

Right: *An early 19th-century ivory thimble holder or needlecase with pinchbeck (or possibly gilt) mount. The holder unscrews to reveal the space where the thimble or needles are contained.*

Below: *A little thimble case of gun metal and brass, charmingly decorated with a horse and rider, designed to hang from a matching chatelaine.*

THIMBLE HOLDERS

Thimble holders, or cases, are delightful objects and desirable to many collectors with or without their contents. It is because of them that so many vintage thimbles are in such excellent condition today, the owner(s) having kept the thimble in its original case, which itself can be quite attractive and decorative. In the eighteenth century, the finest thimbles were often contained in shark-skin (also called shagreen, or *galuchat*), tortoiseshell, ivory or gold cases, with the humbler varieties encased in vegetable ivory, Tartan ware and assorted other materials. The Victorian period is especially rich in unusual thimble holders, with examples shaped like boots and shoes, eggs, suitcases, even ships, with the thimble attached to a mast. Besides the common wooden varieties, thimble holders can be made of pressed glass, leather, porcelain, gilded metal, even mother-of-pearl, the latter two lined with silk or plush.

Left: *A 19th-century (c.1840) filigree silver gilt egg-shaped thimble holder, which was valued at £250 in 1989.*

Right: *Two elaborate 19th-century (c.1880) silver thimble holders with their thimbles. The one on the left is English, and the one on the right Indian, and they were valued in 1990 at £180 and £54 respectively.*

Left: *A silver-plate, rather splendid Victorian goat with a thimble in its saddle. It is grazing on the pins in the pincushion. This was valued in 1990 at £120.*

Above: *A small, painted, wooden, late Victorian thimble holder in the form of a post box.*

Right: *A very rare 1940s Bakelite thimble holder, reminiscent of His Master's Voice. It was sold in 1989 for £58.*

Below: *An unusual selection of 19th-century thimble holders, the most interesting of which is the little pair of binoculars which opens to contain a thimble. The wooden box is Mauchline ware.*

Below: *A 19th-century leather egg-shaped case containing a gold-plated étui, which in turn contains a thimble and a little reel holder.*

Above: *A 19th-century porcelain thimble* **(left)** *with a violet top and forget-me-nots painted around the base, possibly*

French; a very pretty white porcelain thimble **(right)** *with pink rosebuds and leaves and gilt bands top and bottom.*

Above: *Two views of a finely decorated 19th-*

century French gold thimble.

Above: *Three French silver thimbles, the central one possibly steel-topped, and the other two designed*

by Vernon; the thimble on the right is the famous 'Sewing Girls' design.

FRENCH THIMBLES

In the nineteenth century, thimble production in France encompassed gold, silver and the lovely Palais Royal mother-of-pearl types, among others. Thimbles were exhibited at French trade fairs as early as 1819 (in the Palais du Louvre), and in 1834 examples by Mathieu Danloy earned a bronze medal at the Paris Exposition. A. Feau was an established manufacturer specializing in gold and silver thimbles; not only did he display his wares in Paris (in 1878), but he also showed them in Sydney (1879), Melbourne (1880) and Amsterdam (1883). Another well-known French thimble designer was F. P. Laserre, whose creations were sometimes signed 'LAS RRE', the 'RRE' below the 'LAS'.

One of the most renowned silver thimble designers in France was Frederick Charles Victor de Vernon, a metallurgist and sculptor who created thimbles for both P. Lenain & Co. and Maison Duval in Paris. A celebrated Vernon design, in the popular *fin-de-siècle* Art Nouveau style, was known as 'The Sewing Girls': it was illustrated in *Les Modes* in April 1909 and may have been designed to celebrate the marriage of the Dutch Queen Wilhelmina in 1900 (it bears the boar's head mark, for Paris). The thimble of the same design was later produced as part of a leather-boxed sewing set, along with scissors and needlecase, by Maison Duval (one can be seen in the British Museum); it is marked 'J.D.' (for Julian Duval, whose tenure with the firm lasted from 1893 to 1925). Vernon also designed thimbles featuring characters from the famous La Fontaine *Fables* and Perrault's fairy stories, originally dating from the 1890s and reissued *circa* 1910–20 (and again in the United States in the 1970s). Vernon deliberately chose seventeenth-century shapes—complete with waffles—for these sets, since both the fables and fairy tales were written in that century.

Above: **(Right)** *A French thimble, c.1800, in iron with gold or pinchbeck decoration, an exclusively French form of ornamentation.* **(Left)** *A tortoiseshell thimble.*

Above: *French silver thimbles.* (**Left to Right**) *A fairy story thimble, c.1890–1900; another fairy tale, same date; a later copy of the previous design; and a very fine border of raised acorns and twigs, c.1870.*

Above: *Two silver thimbles: on the left is a modern copy of one of the famous "Fable" designs, and on the right, an original from c.1910.*

Unlike English thimbles, whose rims are generally plain, French thimbles of the nineteenth century except for those by Vernon or Lasserre feature decorated rims. Otherwise, French thimbles are usually similar in construction.

The French hallmarking system on needlework tools is called *petite garantie*. A cock appears on gold and silver before 1838 and a rabbit's head on Paris silver from 1819–1838. Parisian silver after 1838 carries a boar's head, provincial silver a crab, and imported goods (of silver or gold) a swan. Gold thimbles after 1838 should bear an eagle's head (or a horse's head, if provincial up to 1919). An owl identifies objects otherwise unmarked from 1893.

Above: *Art Nouveau designs, c.1885–1910.* (**Left to Right**) *A mistletoe border; the fox and the crow; and a fairy tale scene.*

Above: *Two typical 19th-century French designs: on the left, the bouquet of flowers in a basket, and on the right, a love bird on a branch.*

Above: *Late 19th-century European silver thimbles are not always easy to identify: these are probably* (**Left to Right**) *German; French; English; and German.*

PALAIS ROYAL THIMBLES

One of the most desirable thimbles the experienced collector wants to own is a Palais Royal, exquisitely delicate made from mother-of-pearl and named after the palace in Paris originally built in 1629 for Cardinal Richelieu (as the Palais Cardinal) and occupied in the late eighteenth century by the powerful Duc d'Orléans. Members of the duke's entourage required especially luxurious articles for their toilette, travel and other needs, so talented craftsmen in the vicinity of the palace were employed to provide these pieces. Sewing boxes fitted with lovely mother-of-pearl accessories were among the articles made by these workshops, with the thimble usually assuming a dome shape, encircled with two gilt bands at the base. Each sewing tool had a tiny oval plaque containing a blue and green enamel pansy, or sometimes a butterfly, set in gold.

Today it is easier to find individual Palais Royal accessories rather than complete boxes, but remember to look for any cracks in the mother-of-pearl. These thimbles have often lost their oval plaques or had them replaced with a plain gold version, so *caveat emptor*. In fact, there were mother-of-pearl thimbles made with plain gold plaques, but these were usually in the shape of a shield.

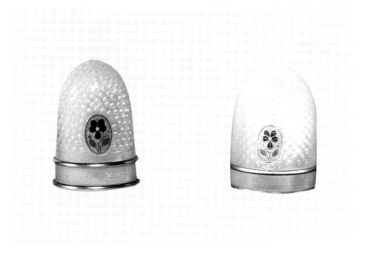

Above: *Two mother-of-pearl Palais Royal thimbles, banded with gilded metal. The one on the left is slimmer than the one on the right but they both have the inserted plaque bearing an enamelled pansy.*

IVORY THIMBLES

Ivory thimbles have long been popular, particularly in France, more perhaps for their delicacy of design than their efficacy in sewing. The earlier ivory thimbles were beehive-shaped, and sometimes finished off with a gilded band. Later varieties often came from China or India, where they were sometimes part of a fitted lacquer or ivory sewing box made for export to Europe. Some of the Oriental thimbles comprise two parts and can be unscrewed, the upper being threaded onto the lower body.

The growing scarcity of ivory in the nineteenth century encouraged the use of corozo or coquilla nuts, both also known as vegetable ivory, for thimbles and other accessories. The former is usually slightly darker than real ivory and has a distinctive, waxy finish, whereas the latter is darker still and was used more for thimble cases. Ironically, vegetable ivory thimbles may cost more than ivory examples as they are difficult to find today.

'Dieppe work' is made of finely carved ivory and derives its name from the French port on the Normandy coast where, as early as the fourteenth century, large quantities of ivory were imported from West Africa. From the seventeenth century, Dieppe carvers were renowned throughout Europe for their fine ivory articles, and such souvenirs were especially popular with Dutch and English tourists. Although sewing items did not comprise the bulk of these carvers' output, there are many examples of carved-ivory pincushions, waxers, shuttles and fans. Small pieces are usually unsigned, although some of their makers imitated medieval craftsmen by carving their 'mark', such as an eye or hand, onto their creations.

Above: *An early 19th-century ivory thimble, made for a child. It is banded with gilded metal.*

Above: *A fine English 19th-century hand painted ivory thimble.*

Above: *A finely carved vegetable ivory thimble.*

Above: *A beautiful ivory thimble showing two ducks as part of a hunting scene.*

BRITISH THIMBLES

In the mid-nineteenth century, Victorian England was at peace, relatively prosperous and at the dawning of the age of the manufactured object. Although the rise of the sewing machine rang the death knell of the common, utilitarian thimble, the production of fancy silver and porcelain models flourished.

SOUVENIR THIMBLES

Hand in hand with rapid industrial growth in Victorian Britain was the rise of public transportation. Railroad lines began to criss-cross and trail up and down the country, taking eager tourists to such places as Windsor Castle, Brighton Pavilion and the Great Exhibition at the Crystal Palace in London's Hyde Park in 1851. The increase in travel and tourism sparked a souvenir trade, and with it the production of the souvenir thimble. Such thimbles might feature portraits of royal residences or pictures of castles, the designs of which were manufactured as ready-made die stamps or as decorated skirts, which were wrapped around the sides before the top was soldered on.

Left: *A souvenir thimble of Brighton Chain Pier.*

Left below: *A souvenir thimble of Lichfield Cathedral, 1850–1860.*

Above: *Two souvenir thimbles: the one above is of Dover Castle.*

Above: *Three souvenirs of Windsor Castle, two on thimbles and one on a finger guard, from c.1840–1850. Souvenir thimbles were very popular at this time.*

Right: *Four souvenir thimbles from the 1850s commemorating the Great Exhibition which opened in Hyde Park, London in 1851 and moved to Sydenham where it reopened in 1854.*

Above: *A superb range of 19th-century souvenir thimbles, including (**Top Row**) a lovely example depicting Lichfield Cathedral on the extreme left, and two different views of Windsor Castle on the right; (**Middle Row**), souvenir thimbles of Dublin, Cheltenham, Dover and Sir Walter Scott's house, Abbotsford; and (**Bottom Row**) four more fine examples, including views of Brighton Pavilion, the Tay Bridge, and Newstead Abbey.*

ENGLISH SILVERSMITHS

Thimbles were made by various silversmiths of the nineteenth century and in great number. Although each thimble may not carry a hallmark (and accompanying initials of the maker), a great many of them do. The following silversmiths and companies were the principal makers of thimbles in Victorian Britain:

Joseph Taylor, Birmingham. While he did not produce large numbers of thimbles during the time he was in business (late eighteenth to early nineteenth century), Taylor made finger-guards and also patented a brass non-slip thimble.

Charles May, London. Firm existed from 1805 to 1929; thimbles usually quite plain.

George Unite, Birmingham. Unite and J. Hillard registered the mark 'G.&H.' on 8 August 1832. Unite's own mark, 'GU', was used 1832–61, and from 1873–90 same mark was used by William Oliver Unite, Edward Wiloughby Unite and George Richard Unite, who traded as George Unite and Sons. 1890–1927, Harry Lyde traded as George Unite & Sons, and the company became George Unite Sons & Lyde in 1928, when the punch 'GUS & L' was adopted (until 1931, when it was cancelled).

Above: *A silver thimble made by MCAS Ltd in Birmingham in 1910, and decorated with a blackberry pattern; the maker's mark is just visible.*

Left: *Three English silver enamelled thimbles, one with pretty flowers on a white band, the second with a pale blue band and the third with flowers on alternating green and black grounds.*

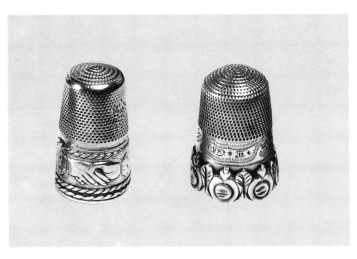

Left: *A 19th-century silver thimble with a silver 'fish' border.*

Middle Left and Far Left: *Two silver 19th-century thimbles, one with a heavily ornamented border and the other with an unusual clasped hands border.*

James Fenton: 1852

James Fenton: 1860

James Fenton: 1868

James Fenton: 1878

James Fenton: 1882

James Fenton: 1911

James Fenton: 1911

Above: *A baby's silver thimble and a Dreema thimble made by Henry Griffiths, marked 'HG&S17'.*

Above: *A selection of James Fenton silvermarks: the first recorded Fenton mark dates from November 1851, and the last recorded mark from December 1923.*

James Fenton, Birmingham. Firm traded from *c*.1850 to 1900. First registered mark in November 1851. Further punches registered between 1860 and 1882. Last entry was for January 1885, and Fenton died in 1886. In March 1885 Fenton's son-in-law Samuel John Boosey became proprietor of firm, trading as James Fenton (continuing same mark). In May 1890 Alan Howard Elkington and Walter Bolding replaced Boosey as proprietors and continued using Fenton mark. Last mark recorded in December 1923.

Henry Griffiths & Sons Ltd., Leamington Spa. Traded from 1886 to 1955. Founder Henry Griffiths worked until 1916, when his sons took over the business and formed a public company. Son Fred, who joined the firm in 1880, is supposed to have given the name 'Dreema', after his daughter, to the popular thimble (which rivalled Charles Horner's Dorcas model). Fred Griffiths died in 1951; firm continued making thimbles until 1955.

Walker & Hall. Manufactured a thimble similar to

Left: (Top Row, Left to Right) *A child's late 19th-century silver thimble, unhallmarked; two Connemarra marble silver stone tops by James Swann.* **(Second Row, Left to Right)** *A maid's thimble unhallmarked, and two thimbles with bicycles on them by James Fenton.* **(Third Row, Left to Right)** *Three thimbles by James Fenton, 1939.* **(Fourth Row, Left to Right)** *Four late 19th-century thimbles, including* **(second from right)** *a fine Henry Griffiths, 1895.*

Dorcas and Dreema, called 'Dura', which is fairly rare today. Yet another manufacturer (unknown today) made the rare sister 'Doris' model.

Joseph Addis. Existed from 1828 to 1885.

James Collins. 1828–70.

James Webb. 1843–90.

Francis Clarke, Birmingham. 1830s.

James Swann. Founded 1890, continues today.

Deacon & Francis, Birmingham. Exists today.

Olney, Amsden & Son. A late nineteenth-century firm, whose mark was 'O.A. & S.'. Makers of the blackberry pattern, among others.

Right: *'Long Live Queen Adelaide', celebrated her coronation in 1831, and was one of the earliest commemoratives ever made.* **Below:** *'The Prince of Wales – Our Future Hope' was struck to celebrate the birth of Queen Victoria's son in 1841.*

COMMEMORATIVE THIMBLES

Silver royal commemoratives became very popular in the nineteenth century: two of the first made for the 1831 coronation of William IV and his wife (one bore the words 'Long live King William IV', the other 'Long live Queen Adelaide'). Numerous commemorative thimbles were issued to celebrate births, marriages and other events connected to Queen Victoria and her family, including her ascension and coronation in 1837 and her marriage to Prince Albert in 1840.

Right: *Three souvenir thimbles commemorating Victoria's coronation and her wedding to Albert.*

Above: *A souvenir thimble struck to record Victoria's coronation.*

Above: *Commemoratives, though created to celebrate specific events and people, also reflect the thimble style of their time, and can complement any general collection, as seen in this fine period group.*

Above: *Four silver commemorative thimbles celebrating, respectively, Victoria's wedding, coronation, silver and Diamond Jubilees.*

Left: *More Victoria Jubileee commemoratives, this time struck in plate: this was one of the most popular 19th-century subjects.*

Above: *Three souvenir thimbles, with various messages, commemorating* **Victoria's wedding to Albert.**

Above: *This imposing Diamond Jubilee thimble (1897) truly captured late Victorian style.*

CHARLES HORNER AND THE DORCAS STORY

Charles Horner, of Hebden Bridge, Yorkshire, and later Halifax, is well known to thimble enthusiasts for his steel-lined thimble, later called Dorcas, which he patented in 1884 (pat. no. 8954). Between 1887 and 1890 many patterns were issued.

The original Dorcas thimbles did not carry the name Dorcas, rather just the Registered Design Number (rd. no.) or pat. (abbreviation for patent). The earlier Dorcas had a domed top, whereas later ones often had flat tops. The Little Dorcas came later; whether the Junior Dorcas was a version of the Little Dorcas, or a later development, is not known.

Charles Horner also made thimbles in solid silver and gold, these bearing the initials 'CH' and usually the Chester assay mark. In 1896 the firm's founder, Charles Horner, died and business was carried on by J.D. and C.H. Horner. The original Dorcas was made until 1905, at which time new, improved Dorcas thimbles were introduced (under the name 'Improved'). The pat. and registered design numbers were later dropped; subsequent thimbles were stamped with the name 'Dorcas', mark 'CH' and size number. By 1925 silver production ceased and only the Dorcas continued in production.

The 'Improved Dorcas' was also made in 9-carat gold with the same steel lining as the silver model. 'Gold Dorcas', 'Little Dorcas' and 'Junior Dorcas' specimens are all extremely rare.

Type	Design
The Shell (rd. no. 210799)	All-over shell or fan design, including top
Princess May (rd. no. 210800)	Daisies inside squares, including top
Plain	Round indentations, including top
Engraved	Engraved border, followed by indentations
Daisy	All-over daisy design
Diamond (rd. no. 73626)	All-over small square design
Star	All-over star design
Louise (rd. no. 127211)	All-over design of flowers (without centres)
Persian	All-over intricate design
Flora	Border of squares, daisies over the top

Right: *Four Dorcas thimbles. The CH stands for Charles Horner, and the number denotes the size. Here are shown (**left to right**) a size 8 star pattern; a size 6 dimple; a size 5 flower and waffle; and a patent waffle pattern.*

Right: (Left to Right) *A souvenir or advertising thimble from Henry Griffiths & Son; two extremely rare 'Little Dorcas' thimbles (all of which were made by Charles Horner); and a size 6 steel-cased Dorcas dimple, with decorated border.*

Above: *Sixteen beautiful silver thimbles, all assayed at Chester. These are all from Charles Horner, unless otherwise noted.* **Top row (left to right)** *An 1898 Louise rim, with border of gold flowers and heart; a 1902 flower border with heart and Princess May pattern top; a 1900 beaded rim, flower and heart border and dimpled top; and a 1905 flat rim, with engraved flowers and double gold band.* **Second row (L-R)** *1910 , Chinese Dragons with dimpling; 1905, Chinese Dragons with Princess May pattern (this by M&C); 1907, cherubs and garlands; 1905, Polygon border of flowers, with dimpling.* **Third row (L-R)** *1903, holly and berries, with shell pattern; 1902, small flowers, with Princess May pattern; 1901, clover leaves with dimpling; 1905, water lilies, with Louise pattern on top.* **Bottom row (L-R)** *1905, Vandyked rim with diamond pattern top; 1904, clover rim with Princess May (this by S&G); 1905, Vandyked rim with Princess May; and 1905, cut Annular rim, with diamond top.*

ENGLISH SILVER HALLMARKS AND OTHER STAMPS

English silver thimbles should always be stamped with a lion, which denotes that the silver is of sterling quality, ie, .925 or 92.5% pure. The next stamped device indicates the town where the article was assayed, the most common being London's leopard's head, Birmingham's anchor, Chester's three corn sheaves and Sheffield's crown. This device is followed by the date letter, which is enclosed within a shield or cartouche and indicates the year of manufacture. These three marks may be followed by the maker's initials. Various highly detailed handbooks can be purchased explaining these terms and identifying the dates represented by the date letter.

Some thimbles also contain registered numbers, which originated from the Patents Design and Trade Marks Act of 1883. The numbers are consecutive from 1883 and reached 600,000 by *c.*1910, allowing for approximately 20,000 designs a year. Thus a thimble with rd. no. 222445 should date from *c.*1893. Remember, however, that the date of the registered design is not always the same as the date of manufacture of that particular thimble.

The Britannia silver quality mark was introduced by William III in 1696 to prevent the coin of the realm from being melted down to make plate. The act forbade the manufacture and hallmarking of plate of sterling (.925) quality. The quality of plate was changed to the higher grade of .958, and the figure of Britannia in profile indicates this higher standard of silver; it is used on coronation commemoratives even today.

AN UNUSUAL REGISTRATION MARK

There is another mark applied to articles that relates to patents, though it is rarely found on thimbles, except for some made for the Great Exhibition of 1851. The mark is a diamond-shaped lozenge and was used in England from 1842 to 1883; it indicates that the design had been lodged with the London Patent Office. In 1884 the diamond mark was superseded by a row of numbers, for example 012345. So if a piece bears the diamond it is from 1883 or earlier; if there is a registered number, it dates from 1884 onward.

Right and Below

Right: *Two groups of four late 19th- and early 20th-century Charles Horner silver thimbles. Three of the thimbles show further variations on the blackberry pattern, one of them with a rather unusual hallmark ('STERLING') for a Charles Horner object of the period. The marks are clearly visible on some of the thimbles, on or just above the rim. There are up to five marks, denoting size, maker, silver quality, assay office, and the date of manufacture.*

BRITISH BASE-METAL THIMBLES

The rise of popularity of the sewing machine meant the beginning of the end of the thimble. Many thimble manufacturers closed down during the nineteenth century, especially those providing 'working thimbles' of base metal to clothing manufacturers. Still, numerous firms survived, or even started up to produce thimbles for industry, among them Edwin Lowe Ltd., a London firm trading from 1852 to the mid-twentieth century. Lowe exported thimbles to the United States and also produced them for the Royal Army Clothing Department. The firm no longer makes thimbles today, although it still exists as a maker of other metal items.

Charles Iles established his firm in 1840 and won an award for his thimbles displayed in London at the 1851 Great Exhibition. He also received prizes at the Kensington Exhibition (1862) and Brussels Exposition (1877). The firm experienced even greater success in the next century, doubling its production by the 1920s and producing aluminium (or alurine), plastic, nickel and chrome-plated thimbles through the 1960s.

Both thimbles and needles by Abel Morrall & Co. were exhibited at the international exposition in London in 1862. The thimbles are marked either 'Abel Morrall' or 'O.A.S.'. Thimble production ceased in the late nineteenth century, but the firm continued to make needles as part of the Aero group.

Left: *Brass working thimbles are not nearly as plain as their name might imply, as these pictures show.* **(Top Row, Left to Right)** *A pretty leaf border, with decorated rim; an Etruscan wave border; a scroll border; and another leaf border.* **(Bottom Row, Left to Right)** *A Flower-wheel border; a zig-zag border with dots; a leaf border; and a Greek key border.*

Below: *This smart group of brass working thimbles—mostly English—indicates the wide range of sizes, shapes, designs, and even colours, developed over the years.*

Above, right and below: *Although the brass and base metal thimble has few claims to individual fame, when displayed in groups such as these, they can be seen to very obviously transcend the merely functional. Some are delightfully light, elegant, and attractive, while others have fascinating historical associations.*

ENGLISH PORCELAIN THIMBLES

English porcelain thimbles experienced unprecedented success in the nineteenth century, and today they are among the most desirable types of thimbles sought by collectors. The richest period for such thimbles is from the late nineteenth to the early twentieth century, although every collector should be familiar as well with the earlier designs, styles and marks (as you never know when you might happen upon a rare treasure). The Worcester factory provided the largest number of thimbles, but it is known that Wedgwood produced at least a small number of thimbles at their Etruria works, though only for about a decade from the late 1790s.

The prolific Royal Worcester porcelain factory was established in the eighteenth century, but its thimble production was greatest in the late nineteenth and early twentieth centuries. Early in the 1800s the Japanese Imari influence (1800–10), exotic-bird designs (1810–1815) and flowers and landscapes (1815–70) were rife, but seldom have these been found on thimbles (although the Smithsonian Institu-

Left: *A blush ground late 19th-century Worcester porcelain thimble, decorated with a yellow-breasted, blue-winged bird, and gilded.* **Below left:** *A very pretty late 19th-century English porcelain thimble depicting a brightly coloured garland of flowers.*

tion in Washington, D.C., owns Worcester thimbles decorated with landscapes). From 1870 to 1930 floral designs continued in use, and there were numerous avian motifs as well. Thimbles with white, blush ivory or peach grounds often feature bird or floral patterns; jewelled patterns featuring droplets of coral and turquoise were also popular. Many of these continued to be made through to the present century, although today thimble production has ceased.

Early Worcester thimbles are not often marked, mainly because of space restrictions, so the collector should become familiar with the detailed brushwork, elaborate gilding and highly translucent porcelain that were so characteristic of the factory. Although nineteenth-century painters were not allowed to sign thimbles, it is known that Read and Hopewell were among Worcester's thimble decorators in the Victorian period. After 1900, signatures began to appear; but only those of qualified painters.

Above: *Two 19th-century English porcelain thimbles, both unmarked. The straight sided white thimble with the rosebud may be a Coalport; and the thimble on the right decorated with a rose is in the style of Worcester.*

Above: *Two 19th-century English porcelain thimbles, both unmarked. The white thimble with brilliant flowers is similar to the late 19th-century enamel thimbles and the straight-sided thimble with rosebuds may be a Coalport.*

Left: *A 19th-century Worcester porcelain thimble with a robin and two gilt bands.*

Right: *Five antique English porcelain thimbles, all with fine quality hand painting.* (**Left to Right**) *A yellow-breasted bird; a yellow-breasted bird with foliage; a red-breasted bird on a blush background; a flower posy on a white ground, c.1860–70; and a pre-hallmark Worcester, c.1870, depicting a black crested bird on a biscuit-coloured ground.*

Right: *Four elegant 'jewelled' Worcester thimbles.* (**Left to Right**) *A peach ground with turquoise droplets; a white ground glazed with turquoise, gold, and white droplets; a peach ground with turquoise droplets; and a white glazed ground with unusual green droplets.*

Right: *A very handsome range of porcelain thimbles, showing bird and butterfly designs.*

Right: *Four fine Worcester thimbles, all of them painted by W. Powell except for the honeysuckle. The thimbles sold for (**Left to Right**) £190; £230; £240; and £190 in the summer of 1988.*

Left: *Five porcelain Worcester thimbles.* **(Left to Right)** *Bird, unmarked, c.1890; robin, unmarked, c.1860; blue tit, purple mark inside, c.1910; bird by Powell, purple mark inside, c.1920–30; bird by Braker, purple mark inside, c.1920–30. Sold 1986 for £170; £190; £170; £190; and £150.*

Left: *Four porcelain Worcester thimbles in perfect condition.* **Left to Right:** *Bird by Mosley; blue tit by Powell; another Mosley; and a 'jewelled' thimble, unmarked, c. 1890. The three signed thimbles all carry the purple mark inside, and are c.1920-30. The thimbles sold for £150; £190; £150; and £250 in 1986.*

Left: *Four porcelain Worcester thimbles.* **(Left to Right)** *Blue tit by E. Barker; yellow bird by Powell; blue-green bird by Powell; and red-breasted bird by Mosley. All contain the purple mark; they were sold in late summer 1986 for £150; £190; £190; and £150 respectively.*

Left: *Five hand painted Worcester thimbles.* **(Left to Right)** *Kingfisher by S. Oram, c.1970; gold crest by W. Powell, c. 1930s; blackcap by W. Powell, c.1930s; blue tit by W. Powell, c.1920; and peaches and grapes by M. Igoe, c.1970. Sold in Spring 1987 for £16; £190; £190; £190; and £14.*

The late nineteenth-century Worcester thimbles that are marked contain a puce mark indicating that they were made after 1891. The puce mark gave way to a black mark after 1938. The factory did use a dating code from 1862 through the 1960s, but it was seldom applied to thimbles. Rather, a special small mark was used for the thimbles, though it was not altered every year.

The only other English factories producing Victorian porcelain thimbles that can be identified were in Derby. The Bloor Derby factory closed down in 1848, but its former employees started up the firm Stevenson & Hancock soon after; the factory operated until 1935. The mark 'S&H' is found inside some but not all of these Derby thimbles. Another Derby factory made thimbles as well, the Royal Crown Derby Porcelain Company, which in fact took over Stevenson & Hancock in 1935.

Above: *A highly decorated pair of English 19th-century porcelain thimbles, each incorporating flower motifs together with embellishment and gilding.*

Left: *A striking group of English porcelain thimbles. (**Left to Right**) A Worcester holly design, which has a robin on the reverse; a rare Derby Imari pattern; a very fine Worcester "jewelled" thimble, c.1880; and another elegant English 19th-century design.*

Left: *Four 19th-century porcelain thimbles including a Worcester (second from right) and a Derby bearing the Stevenson and Hancock S&H mark inside (extreme right).*

<table>
<tr><td>

'Peeps' or Stanhopes

'Peepshow' thimbles, or 'peeps', were made between 1860 and 1930, and are sometimes known as Stanhopes (after the third Earl of Stanhope, who purportedly invented the Stanhope magnifying lens in the eighteenth century). Peepshow thimbles were patented in Britain by William Pursall in 1880, and exploited the development of microphotography for commercial purposes, recessing a tiny photograph into the top of a thimble and placing a magnifying lens above it. Such thimbles are necessarily novelty items, unsuited for practical use. They are large and awkward because of the need to protect the image and the lens, and few examples have survived. Consequently they command high prices. Typical photographic images contained in these thimbles feature tourist resorts or portraits of Queen Victoria and other members of the royal family.

</td></tr>
</table>

GERMAN THIMBLES

The most prominent nineteenth-century thimble manufacturer in Germany was Johann Ferdinand Gabler, a tailor's son born in 1778. Gabler started up the business in 1825 and it reached its peak in 1914, when Gebrüder Gabler employed some 150 workers. The firm produced gold, silver, brass, nickel and aluminium thimbles over the years. Early Gabler thimbles are sometimes marked with a 'G' in a rosette, whereas some later models incorporate an eight-pointed star-shaped pattern at the top; some, however, were not marked. Competition was fierce among German thimble makers, so designs and marks were often copied, among them Gabler's star-shaped top.

Gabler manufactured hundreds of different types of thimbles, with such elements as enamelling, shields, initials, stone tops or stone skirts added to the basic shape. Some late nineteenth-century examples were decorated with curvilinear Art Nouveau (or Jugendstil, as it was known in Germany) motifs. Gabler thimbles were available in .925 or lower-grade silver, the cheaper type giving Gabler and other German firms an edge in the export trade, but in general lowering the overall quality of output. Some of Gabler's top-quality thimbles entered the Russian Royal Collection,

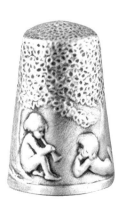

Above: *A beautifully displayed and very carefully assembled group of German silver thimbles of the period 1880–1910.*

Above: *Two views of a child's 19th-century silver thimble.*

Right: *A group of 19th-century German thimbles, almost certainly made for the Italian export market. Their skirts are set with precious stones in very ornate skirts, but the upper parts are comparatively plain.*

Right: *A French (extreme left) and four German 19th-century thimbles made of brass and silver. The thimble bearing the legend 'Forget Me Not' was made for the export markets.*

whereas the majority of them were intended for the general market.

The Gabler thimbles that were exported to Russia include models with often carry the Russian hallmark of '84' or '88' on their rim, but they should not be confused with indigenous Russian examples. Likewise, exports to Scandinavia were marked with assorted hallmarks of those countries, thus making for at times confusing similarities between thimbles coming out of Germany, Russia and Scandinavia during this period.

Among the other German thimble makers were Frederich Eber of Pforzheim, a firm that existed until 1980; Soergel & Stollmeyer of Schwabisch-Gmund; Helmut Greif of Winterbach and Wilhelm Lotthammer of Pforzheim. The latter firm operated from 1850 to 1969, and published its catalogue under the name of Lotthammer & Stutzel. Windmills and country scenes of blue and white enamel often appear

Left: *A 19th-century German thimble, hallmarked '84', indicating that it was made for the Russian export market.*

on Lotthammer's silver thimbles, mistakenly suggesting to many collectors a Dutch origin. However, the star-petal top indicates German manufacture, and the windmill-decorated versions were probably made for export.

Lutz & Weiss, Eber & Pranol and the Johann Moritz Rump company all produced thimbles in Germany in the nineteenth century but only Rump does so today. In 1845, Rump produced 12,000 gross metal thimbles! The firm has recently published a booklet illustrating its early thimble designs.

Few porcelain thimbles are known to have been made in nineteenth-century Germany.

AUSTRIAN THIMBLES

The most distinctive nineteenth-century thimbles made in Austria were attractive silver examples with raised decoration. Many of these were unmarked, but those that were marked included a number on the front indicating the 'Loth', that is, the standard unit of silver purity used in Germany, Austria and much of central Europe. The numbers '12' and '13' represented .725 and .825, respectively. This system of marking was discontinued c.1860.

Above: *A selection of 19th-century thimbles carrying the '84' hallmark. These are notoriously difficult to attribute, but this group is probably all from the Gabler factory.*

Above: *Four silver and enamel thimbles, including a Charles Horner commemorative for the accession of King Edward VIII (1936), and three German examples, the two with windmills designed for export to The Netherlands.*

Below: *A very nice 19th-century Austrian silver thimble. The mark '800' on the front describes the quality of the silver.*

Right: *A beautiful tall, slim, engraved 19th-century Scandinavian gold thimble with a moonstone top. The engraving has an almost Celtic style.*

Below right: *This group, c.1870–80, illustrates some of the distinctive styles and finishes produced by Scandinavian thimble makers. Of particular interest is the gold thimble, third from the left, with moonstone top, and the three crown emblem of Sweden.*

Below: *A striking arrangement of Norwegian silver gilt and enamel thimbles from the late 19th and early 20th centuries. Those with plain colours and scenes from life are later in date than those with geometric or curvilinear patterns.*

NORWEGIAN THIMBLES

Of the Scandinavian countries, which generally imported thimbles from abroad, Norway evolved its own distinctive gold and silver thimbles, some with stone tops and finely engraved straight sides, others enamelled, others undecorated. Enamelled thimbles were a Norwegian speciality, with early silver and silver-gilt examples sporting enamelled border designs and later examples, such as those by the Oslo silversmith David Andersen, decorated with reindeer, polar bears and fjord scenes. Some of Andersen's older thimbles have moonstone tops, with enamelling covering guilloche-style, engine-turned silver, whereas examples from the twentieth century have silver-gilt waffle-shaped tops. The Andersen firm still produces enamelled thimbles today.

Left: *A late 19th-century Russian thimble and case in silver and applied silver from the Caucasus region.*

RUSSIAN THIMBLES

Russian thimbles generally fall into one of three distinctive styles, niello, enamel and a form of applied cut card work. Souvenir thimbles from the Caucasus often bore names in Cyrillic script and were decorated in the niello style, wherein a black design is etched onto a silver background. Such thimbles are not as costly as the famous Russian enamel thimbles, on which polychrome enamel is laid between little wire reserves on a ground of silver-gilt or gold. The finest enamel thimbles demonstrate subtle variations of shading, such as the light pink on the inside of a flower blossom darkening at the edge of the petals.

Not all Russian silver thimbles are hallmarked but if they are, the hallmark is found on the rim with either '84' or '88'. Until 1925 the Slothnik was the Russian unit of purity applied to silver, with 96 representing pure silver. From 1896 to 1907 a woman's head facing left was sometimes used on Russian silver, and from 1908 to 1917 a woman's head facing right, but such marks are rare on thimbles. After 1927 the '84' changed to '88' or '.875'.

The more marks on a piece of Russian silver, the more important that piece, so four marks—for instance, '84', the factory name, the town where it was

Above: *A thimble from the Caucasus with Cyrillic script.*

Above: *A fine late 19th-century Russian silver thimble. The mark on the rim is the Kokoshnik mark, a woman's head facing to the left. The initials 'I.W.' in Cyrillic script are the maker's mark.*

made and the maker's initials—denote a significant item of silver. The size of thimbles, however, precluded the use of many marks, and the number alone is found most frequently. Beware, however, of recent copies or fakes bearing the '84' on their rim; the workmanship on such thimbles is usually quite poor.

Left: *A gorgeous array of extremely fine, ornate Russian enamel thimbles, showing some of the colours and decorative styles developed.*

AMERICAN THIMBLES

Production of thimbles in the United States reached its zenith at the end of the nineteenth century. In general, thimbles of this period retained their shorter shape of the eighteenth century, the only changes being apparent in their indentations, which became larger and assumed a uniform roundness. Most American thimbles from this time exhibit both a firm grasp of design and quality workmanship, although they were less variable in design than their European counterparts. Silver examples from 1860 onwards usually bear the word 'STERLING' or 'STERLING SILVER'.

Porcelain thimbles were not widely produced in North America in the nineteenth century, but collectors should be on the lookout for the factory names Ott and Brewer and also the Ceramic Art Company, both from New Jersey and both of which manufactured porcelain thimbles at the end of the century. Notable American thimble manufacturers included the following firms:

Simons Brothers & Company, Philadelphia. George Washington Simons founded his company in 1839 in Philadelphia although it was not to be named Simon bros. for over 40 years. George, his brother and his four sons ran their business from the Old Jones Hotel —which they refurbished and renamed the Artisan Building—in Chestnut Street from 1864. The company won a medal for their excellent thimbles at the 1876 Centennial Exposition in Philadelphia.

Simons Bros. thimbles are marked with a Gothic S inside an upturned bell or shield, a mark they had used from the 1880s onwards but did not register until 1907. It appears on both their gold and silver thimbles and is still current today. A smaller trademark generally indicates an earlier thimble. Simons Bros. have reissued their thimbles for collectors, and the reissues, some of them dating from the 1890s, and made from the original dies, are almost as sought after as the first issues of the same models.

Ketcham & McDougall Company, New York. Existed from 1832 (when it was founded as Prime & Roshore) to 1932 as jewellers. Hugh McDougall joined the Ketcham firm, located in New York, in 1857, although it was not until 1875 that the partnership between him and Edward Ketcham was formed (prompting the change of name to Ketcham & McDougall). The company produced a variety of items including thimbles which were marked with the MKD trademark from its introduction in August 1892. Some of the earlier thimbles carry the patent mark 'Sep 20, 81'. Ketcham & McDougall made thimbles from many metals including steel, silver and gold and were the first American company to market aluminium thimbles. They stopped making thimbles in 1932.

P. W. Lambert & Company, New York. They produced oxidized silver and 'Egyptian Gold' thimbles, chatelaines, ladies' belts and other goods from the middle of the nineteenth century onwards.

Untermeyer-Robbins. Existed from 1890 to 1930, after which time it was bought by Stern. Mark 'UR'.

Stern Brothers and Company. Operated from 1868–1933. The Stern family emigrated from Munsingen in Germany, arriving in Philadelphia in 1863. Nathan Stern worked for Henry Muhr and Sons before starting his own business at 63 Nassau Street, New York. The Stern Bros. catalogue in 1890 advertized a complete list of thimbles: these bore the company trademark of an anchor with a rope twisted around it from 1890–1908. Collectors will recognize later thimbles by their trademarks: an 'S' with a 'B' in its upper curve and a 'C' in its lower curve was used on thimbles from 1908–12. A 'G' enclosing an 'S' and a 'C' marks thimbles produced between 1913 and 1933, the 'G' representing August Goldsmith who had become a partner. The stock market crash of 1929 hit Stern Bros. badly and the business shut down in 1933.

Waite Thresher Company Limited, Providence, Rhode Island. Daniel Waite established himself as a silversmith in Providence, in 1860 and was joined by a new partner, Henry Thresher, in 1884. Their early thimbles (c.1886–c.1906) are marked with a star inside the top; later thimbles (c.1907–c.1927) are marked with a thimble inside a star. Waite Thresher stopped making thimbles in 1927 and sold their designs and machinery to Simons Bros.

H. Muhr and Sons, Philadelphia. Operated from 1873–1894. Mark: a crown.

Nineteenth-century American thimbles are perhaps underpriced in comparison with English thimbles and this is a good time therefore for collectors to look for interesting items to add to their collection. Good American thimbles can often be bought for less in Europe than in the United States of America.

Left: *The sixteen thimbles shown on this page are all from the famous Simons Brothers and Company, of Philadelphia. The range of work illustrated here reinforces the point that American thimbles have a tendency to be stylistically different from their European equivalents; rather less variable in design and ornamentation, they also retained the stubbier, shorter shape while European thimbles were growing taller and slimmer.*

Right: *Four attractive examples from the production of Ketcham and McDougall. The company prospered greatly in the later years of the 19th century, but ceased thimble production in 1932.*

Right: *Four American silver thimbles.* **(Left to Right)** *A Stern Brothers thimble made by August Goldsmith c.1913–27, decorated with flowers in panels; a Muhr thimble with grapes; another Goldsmith thimble of a similar date; and a size 9 with wheatsheafs and a crown trademark.*

Right: *Four Stern silver thimbles, 1908–12.* **(Left to Right)** *A raised diamond pattern with anchor on the outside; Art Nouveau pattern with anchor on the outside; size 6 'propellor' pattern with anchor on the outside; and size 7 with anchor inside the top.*

Right: *Four Waite Thresher silver thimbles.* **(Left to Right)** *A pre-1913 lobed leaf pattern; a folk art pattern, 1913–27; a dogwood flower, 1913–27; and a thimble with a gilded band and a small ring for suspension.*

THIMBLES FROM THE NEAR AND FAR EAST

Occasionally nineteenth-century thimbles from Armenia, India, China and other oriental countries become available in the West. Examples from Afghanistan, for instance, have come out of that country of late. Such thimbles are usually worn by women as jewellery, either attached to a finger ring or worn under their head veils.

Armenian thimbles of silver or gold with black niello-type decoration are known, and black and silver niello thimbles have come from the Mesopotamian region (in present-day Iran and Iraq).

India produced handsome repoussé silver and gold thimbles in the 1800s, many versions with scalloped or waved edges. Such decorated thimbles were imported by the British Army & Navy Stores, and were also intended for the domestic market, primarily for the British Raj in India. Some British firms even copied elaborate Indian designs, and there are cases of Indian-made thimbles receiving English hallmarks.

Antique shops in Hong Kong have yielded silver or enamelled silver sewing rings; some of these have been authenticated as nineteenth-century antiques by specialists in Chinese enamelling and silver design. silver design.

Above and above left: *Two Armenian thimbles, an early 19th century iron example with gold inlay (left), and a 19th-century silver design (right).*

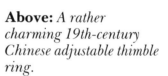

Above: *A rather charming 19th-century Chinese adjustable thimble ring.*

Left: *An unusual group of Chinese sewing rings, c.1870–80, some of which are adjustable.*

Above: *A 19th-century Persian silver thimble, decorated with a pattern of roses and peacocks, and with a waffle top.*

Right: *Two very nice 19th-century silver thimbles: the one on the right is Tunisian, and the one on the left is Armenian.*

Right: *Two late 19th- or early 20th-century Afghani thimble and ring sets.* **Below:** *An early 19th-century gold thimble set with garnets, found in Afghanistan.*

Right: *Four 19th-century silver Afghani thimbles with exotic design motifs.* **Below right:** *Two more thimble and ring sets: these were decorative and ornamental, like jewellery, as well as practical and functional.*

Left: *Three deliciously elaborate silver designs. The one on the extreme left is certainly Indian, c.1880; the provenance of the other two is less certain, but if not themselves Indian, their design is clearly heavily influenced by the region.*

Left: *Four silver and stone thimbles.* **(Left to Right)** *Turquoise and coral; turquoise with a scalloped edge; turquoise, possibly Turkish; and a thimble with pale blue enamel band and a pink flower.*

Left: *Four silver thimbles, late 19th- or early 20th-century, the one on the left showing 'England', the others possibly Turkish.*

Left: *A group of late 19th-century thimbles, possibly Indian, with a variety of designs with figures in relief; the second thimble from the right bears the date 1896.*

Left: *Five 19th-century Indian silver thimbles, all with very strong designs; the central three have scalloped rims.*

TWENTIETH-CENTURY THIMBLES

During the twentieth century, mass-production

has played an increasing role in everyday life.

The availability of cheap materials has led to

an explosion in the numbers of thimbles being

made, and although few mass-produced

examples will become the 'antiques of

tomorrow', hand-crafted and commemorative

thimbles will enhance any collection.

After the turn of the century, Art Deco was all the rage. The 1920s planted the seeds of modern living, and mass production played an ever-increasing role in everyday life. The German equivalent of the Art Deco movement, the Jugendstil, was running its own course of modernization in Europe. The mass-production of aluminium (or, to give it its older name, alurine) thimbles was developed for advertizing purposes, with the thimbles employed as a give-away token (Iles and Gomme have recently decided to reissue certain aluminium advertizing thimbles through a mail-order catalogue in Great Britain), and the twentieth century saw the growing invention of the gadget thimble, usually made in cheap metal. The nickel finger-shaped thimble was patented in England by H. Bourne in 1904, and led on to the 'Trueform' thimble which ws made in silver, brass, nickel and later in plastic. Other gadget thimbles included the threader thimble, an aid to pulling the thread through the needle; the magnet top, used to pick up pins and needles; and the ventilated thimble, with ivorine lining.

Left: *Four 1930s advertising thimbles in aluminium, with bands of coloured enamel — including the News of the World, Lyons', and the Evening News.*

Left: *A group of colourful European advertising thimbles, probably c.1940.*

Left: *A group of 20th-century thimbles, including advertising thimbles from Germany, England, and Scotland.*

Below: *Two silver plate 'Trueform' thimbles, c.1905. The thimble on the left bears the patent number 19157.*

Right: *Four English silver advertising thimbles, made by James Swann and Henry Griffiths, and dating from the 1930s. These were given away by James Walker, the London jeweller, with wedding rings, and were very well known at the time.*

Above: *Three silver souvenir thimbles: 'York'; 'Minehead'; and 'Teignmouth', by Henry Griffiths, c.1930 and 'Polly', by James Fenton.*

Above: *Three advertising thimbles, 1926–7, for J. W. Cassidy, and James Walker, and Conroy Couch, of Torquay. On the right is 'James Walker Wishes You Luck'.*

Left: *Two 1920–30 Bakelite or plastic thimbles with cupids and blackbirds around them – popular devices for remembrance.*

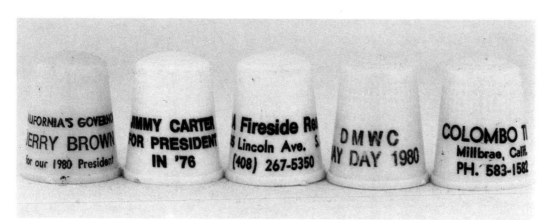

Left: *Five American plastic advertising and election campaign thimbles. The lettering on the thimbles is* **(Left to Right)** *green on yellow; green on cream; brown on cream; brown on pink; and brown on pink.*

Right: *Four charming Spode thimbles, with a pleasing shape, well gilded tops and decoration, and prettily coloured subjects (birds and butterflies).*

Right: *Modern hand painted porcelain.* **(Left to Right)** *Mr Russell painted the first two; and Mr Delaney painted the very fine fruit thimble and the bird. Well conceived and finely hand painted modern thimbles such as these are worth collecting.*

Above: *Four fine modern thimbles.* **(Left to Right)** *The first two are porcelain, made exclusively for the Thimble Society of London, in a limited edition of 100. The second pair are modern Limoges.*

Above: *Four modern hand painted English thimbles.* **(Left to Right)** *Turquoise 'jewelling' on 22-carat gold; fruit in a rich 22-carat gold* cartouche on a very dark blue ground; a bird with a red crest; and turquoise 'jewelling' on a white and 22-carat gilt ground.*

Left: *Four very recent modern English Christmas thimbles.* **(Left to Right)** *Caverswall, 1988; Spode, 1982; Sutherland China, 1981; and a humorous man with a Christmas pudding, again by Spode.*

Below: *A hand painted, hand gilded egg-shaped thimble case, silk-lined in pink with pansy and scroll decorations. The case and its matching thimble and needlecase are all Limoges (French porcelain).*

Celluloid has also been employed in the manufacture of thimbles since the last years of the nineteenth century; some are of solid celluloid while others have celluloid linings; the non-slip celluloid thimble was patented *c.* 1936.

The 1960s and '70s saw the mass-production of inexpensive china thimbles with transfer prints to meet the demands of the booming travel and tourist industries. Although those souvenirs are interesting, they should not be mistaken for antique hand-painted thimbles, nor looked on as an investment.

Many companies have discontinued the manufacture of porcelain thimbles (among them Spode, Wedgwood and Royal Worcester). Less reputable entrepreneurs have sought to exploit the collector's love of the subject and the market has been infested with special issues and collectors' sets of thimbles that have little value, intrinsic or otherwise.

Advertisements can be seductive but the point to look for is whether the design is hand-painted or printed: if it is printed then the thimble is unlikely to be well finished and equally unlikely to appreciate in value. If an advertisement does not clearly state that

Left: *A modern English china thimble by Wedgwood, 1986. A praying female figure is picked out in white relief against a blue background.*

Right: *Various 20th-century commemoratives celebrating events in the lives of King George and Queen Mary. The range of materials here is of interest, with thimbles in plate, brass, and silver.*

Above: *A very well preserved plate commemorative thimble celebrating the marriage of Edward and Alexandra in 1902.*

Right: *20th-century commemoratives celebrating Queen Elizabeth.* **(Left to Right)** *Her coronation in silver plate; her coronation in silver, decorated with an ornate band and a coach and horses motif; the same event recorded in gold; and another coronation piece.*

Right: *An interesting group of modern hand painted thimbles.* **(Left to Right)** *A portrait of Mrs Thatcher on the extreme left; a Mexican or American Indian sterling silver thimble inlaid with blue enamel; a hand painted bird on bone china; and a hand painted blue tit.*

Above: *A handsome silver plate thimble commemorating the coronation of Edward VII.*

Left: *A fine thimble commemorating the Wembley exhibition of 1924; the design and the magnificent lion device have a strong Art Deco influence.*

Left: *Three souvenir thimbles commemorating Her Majesty the Queen's 60th birthday in 1986. The thimbles on the left and right show the front and reverse of the same design; the front reads 'The Queen's 60th Birthday', and the reverse shows a Tudor rose. The thimble in the middle is sterling silver.*

the thimble is hand-painted, call the manufacturer before you part with any money. Most contemporary china thimbles are rarely likely to prove a good buy if you are collecting for profit, as well as pleasure. Be warned: a huge collection of mass-produced modern thimbles, which had been advertized for sale in limited editions as 'antiques of the future' and assembled by their owner at a cost of over £2400 ($4000), recently sold for only £200 ($330).

Some modern thimbles are well worth purchasing however. Good craftsmen and artists deserve to be supported. As a general rule, modern commemoratives are always worth buying. Silver commemoratives have the advantage of a hallmark which identifies when they were made; fine hand-crafted silver and porcelain thimbles as beautiful as any are still being made and can be collected.

Left: *Three brightly coloured modern glass thimbles.*

Right: (Left to Right) *A pewter peep with the peep in the end showing Shakespeare's family house at Stratford-on-Avon; a well-cut modern brass thimble with a sparkling leaf pattern; and a modern brass peep with the peep in the end showing a full-length figure of Queen Victoria.*

Above: *A modern Tunbridge thimble in beige and brown stick ware.*

Below left: *Five attractive modern commemorative peeps, celebrating* (**Left to Right**) *four generations of Queen Victoria's family; the Australian Bicentennial; the Duchess of Windsor's jewels; the same subject, but in brass and blue lacquer, rather than silver; and Queen Elizabeth and Prince Philip's ruby wedding. It is interesting to note that modern peeps view from outside the thimble inwards; genuinely old and antique peeps always view from the inside of the thimble out.*

MAINTENANCE AND CONSERVATION

Once you have started to collect thimbles, you will certainly ask yourself what you should do to look after them and whether you should restore them.

Before you take a thimble to another collector, a dealer or a museum, you may be tempted to clean it, whether because you want to sell it, have it valued, or have it identified if you are uncertain of its origin and date. My general advice is to leave well alone.

Thimble restoration should be undertaken only by experts, most of whom will decline to attempt extensive repair and restoration work because heavily restored thimbles can look so much less attractive and their value is little enhanced if not actually reduced. Of course, the value of a restored thimble will never be the same as that of a perfect example. Good restoration work can be very expensive and the cost may be out of all proportion to the value of the thimble itself.

You will not need the services of a professional if the damage to your thimble is minor only.

IVORY (AND TORTOISESHELL) THIMBLES
Marks left on ivory by sticky labels or general dirt can easily be removed with impregnated wadding used to clean silver or brass. Never use a cleaner mixed with water – it will destroy the sheen. After you have rubbed the dirt off, restore the shine to the thimble with almond oil and buff it with a soft cloth. Tortoiseshell is best treated with almond oil and a soft cloth only. You will not be able to remove the yellow stains found on ivory – these are best tackled only by an expert who will probably have to bleach them off very carefully.

Another tip for cleaning ivory is to make a paste of whitening and lemon juice: rub this on the thimble and leave it to dry before removing the paste. Finally, polish the thimble with a soft cloth. Never clean ivory, bone, alabaster and other thimbles made of porous substances with detergent (which usually contains a mild bleaching agent) and water as you will remove the finish.

Chips and cracks on these thimbles are best left alone altogether unless you can find a restorer who specializes in ivory or tortoiseshell. Both materials can be professionally polished to remove surface scratches.

Ivory and tortoiseshell are affected by changes in temperature and can crack if the air is too dry; always put a glass of water near them. Ivory should be exposed to daylight occasionally to stop it from yellowing, although not in direct sunlight.

BRASS, STEEL AND COPPER THIMBLES
Modern cleaning agents can be used to clean nineteenth-century brass and copper. Earlier pieces, medieval thimbles for example, should not be cleaned.

The old patina should always be retained. Repairs to early metal thimbles are not advisable either.

Steel thimbles should be handled as little as possible as they are particularly vulnerable to rust – even the perspiration from fingers is enough to affect them. Rust can be retarded, if not prevented altogether, by rubbing some lubricating oil lightly onto the thimble. Cotton gloves should be worn if you are going to handle these thimbles frequently. Steel thimbles can be cleaned and polished by professionals, but it is expensive and they can end up looking very new with a rather flat appearance. Collectors look for the original bluish sheen and sparkling cut facets and will pay more for it.

SILVER THIMBLES

Do not use silver dip to clean a silver thimble with a gilt lining or any gilt decoration; if you immerse it in the dip you will plate it with the residue of silver collected in the dip and you will not be able to remove this plating. Avoid all silver cleaning compounds with even the smallest chrome content: although it will help to retard tarnishing, it will also plate the silver. If you have made this mistake, take your silver to a professional silver restorer who will be able to clean it up again.

The wholesale repair of silver thimbles is certainly best left to professionals. Repairing damage to holes requires the removal of all stones beforehand as the thimble has to be heated to a very high temperature. Such heat will destroy any enamelled decoration or niello work. The repair process will also remove the patina on the thimble and the silver will need oxidizing to regain its antique appearance.

Re-plating a silver or gold surface onto a base metal is usually possible. Remove all stones from a stone-set thimble and any padding (in the case of a thimble holder) before immersing the item in the plating solution. You will end up with a very new-looking thimble. If you wish to re-plate only one piece of a set of sewing items, take the whole set to a professional silver restorer who will be able to match the colour for you.

Silver-plating solutions can be bought fairly easily and work reasonably well if applied to a copper base but less well on brass. Such solutions need to be applied many times before the right appearance is obtained, but even then the plating is more likely to wear off than permanent plating undertaken by a professional.

Lead solder was often used to repair old silver. Any attempt to remove it may cause the item to disintegrate.

GOLD THIMBLES

Gold jewellery dip solutions can be bought and used to clean up gold thimbles. Thimbles set with porous stones such as turquoise, coral or pearl should not be immersed in such a solution; hard stones such as diamonds, sapphires and rubies, though, will come to no harm. All stones must be removed if repair work

involves heating. Gold-plating costs at least twice as much as silver-plating and you will need to match the colour closely; there are at least four different colours of gold, rose, green, yellow and 'white'. (The colour of gold bears no relationship to its carat.)

The repair of a hole in the knurling of a gold (or silver) thimble must be done by a professional restorer and will be very expensive because the pattern of the knurling is so difficult to reproduce.

PORCELAIN AND GLASS THIMBLES

Porcelain thimbles may have firing cracks: these are different from hairline cracks and they arise when the clay splits slightly during the firing process. Hairline cracks can develop from firing cracks so thimbles damaged in this way need particularly careful handling. Hairline cracks can be disguised to some extent by slight bleaching but this can damage painted motifs which will then have to be cleaned up and re-painted. If your thimbles are valuable, it is better not to restore them unless your restorer is an artist.

Local ceramic restorers may be a good option for repair work on porcelain thimbles which cannot be washed because this may damage their painted surfaces and glazing.

Those of you lucky enough to have a glass thimble containing a minute scent bottle may have trouble removing the stopper. Put a few drops of lubricating oil around the neck of the bottle and leave it for at least a day – it may be necessary to repeat this process a number of times before you can finally loosen the stopper. A few drops of methyl alcohol can be used instead, to remove any vestiges of perfume, before the stopper is eased out. If both of these methods fail, immerse the bottle top in hot water: the heated air inside the bottle will expand and help to push the stopper out. Do not bend over the bottle to see what is happening as you may get a black eye. Use a wooden clothes peg – never metal pliers which will cause chipping – if you must, to loosen the stopper.

Chips and rough edges on glass thimbles can be ground down to a smooth finish; cracks and breaks cannot be disguised though.

WOODEN THIMBLES

Do not attempt to clean painted wooden thimbles. They are protected by a thin layer of varnish (or less) which is their only defence against the elements. Dust them gently, but no more. Wooden thimbles are also affected by humidity and temperature changes: sensible storage and display are the best ways to limit damage. Try to avoid placing such thimbles in rooms that undergo great changes in temperature or under very strong, hot lighting.

Papier-mâché sewing boxes can be cleaned and their sheen restored with a paste made up of flour and almond oil. Leave the paste to dry and then rub it off gently. A silicon furniture spray or plain beeswax can also be used.

CATALOGUING AND PHOTOGRAPHING A COLLECTION

Unfortunately, thimble collections may begin to attract the attention of burglars. No longer do they take only videos, televisions and stereo cassette players: many antiques and collectables are now regarded as worth stealing. They are also difficult to trace. It is certainly worth keeping an up-to-date catalogue of your collection, preferably with a photograph of each of your thimbles. These will help both you and the police to find them and provide the basis of any insurance claim you wish to make. You should also consider marking your thimbles with your postcode or zip code in an ultra-violet-visible ink. Numbering your thimbles is a good idea. Numbers should be written on sticky-backed labels if they are to be applied to porcelain or other porous materials such as ivory; otherwise numbers can be written directly onto metal thimbles with metal marker pens.

Your catalogue will be both an invaluable record if you are burgled and a very useful means of showing other collectors and dealers the type and range of thimbles in your collection: you will not have to carry your whole thimble collection round with you wherever you go. The compilation of a catalogue makes good sense and is satisfying in itself.

It is easiest to make your catalogue up as your collection grows. A large ring-bound folder is a very convenient way of keeping records: each time you buy, sell or swap an item you can add or remove a page at will without interfering with the rest of the catalogue – this is much more difficult if you have a conventional bound book. The entry for each thimble should mention its type (the material of which it is made), its size, any hallmarks or distinguishing features, its probable place and date of manufacture, any damage or flaws

and anything you know about its previous ownership. You should also keep a 'little black book' which matches your main book and lists when, where and from or to whom you bought or sold all your thimbles. You can keep all of your receipts in it too. For obvious reasons, you should conceal this book in a safe place.

Each thimble should ideally be illustrated with at least two photographs, since group shots of many thimbles together will not be particularly revealing of the fine distinguishing embellishments and ornaments on them. Thimbles of the same materials, design and date can however be photographed with each other and look very attractive together in pictures; group shots can also allow you to compare different designs immediately and conveniently. The major difficulty in such group shots is to get all the thimbles in focus.

Your photographs should show the thimbles' most notable features, 'front' and 'back' and perhaps inside, as well. It is of course up to the individual collector how much detail she or he wishes to show in the photographs. Ensure that you have sufficient depth of field to get the whole of your thimble in focus. You will need to stop down to F16 and may also have to use a light-sensitive 'fast-film'.

Thimbles are quite small objects and require photographing as close up as possible, with carefully positioned lighting; good natural daylight is best. Photograph them against plain or simple coloured backgrounds. Metal thimbles, silver especially, can be adequately photographed using black-and-white film and may even look better in black-and-white than in

colour; the highly polished finish of some metal thimbles militates against using very strong lighting which can often be reflected and obscure the detail. Attention paid to lighting and positioning is always repaid with better photographs.

Photographs will provide you with a record of your collection year by year and are useful in obtaining an up-to-date valuation. Valuations can be had from reputable thimble dealers and auction houses: all you need to do is take the relevant photograph in with any other information you may have and the expert in question will provide you with a free verbal valuation. You will, however, have to pay some nominal fee if you require a valuation for insurance purposes. Many collectors are unaware of this service and more should take advantage of it. Reputable dealers and auction houses enjoy offering this service as it keeps them up

cork cut and stuck at intervals along the shelves to stop your thimbles wobbling each time the 'door' is opened.

Glass domes fitted over round mounting shelves can be placed at either end of a mantelpiece, the domes themselves sitting on wood or lacquer bases stained or painted to suit the room. A glass-topped coffee table can be placed over a shallow showcase with thimbles on their side: use coloured putty or children's plasticine to hold them in place.

Cotton reel drawers from an old sewing cabinet are ideally partitioned for thimble display; these can be bought in antique markets or occasionally picked up from stores undergoing complete re-fitting and re-furbishing. Printers' wooden trays also make attractive display units. These can be fitted with a glass or perspex door with light brass hinges, when used upright, or laid flat on a made-to-measure wrought iron or brass coffee table frame and then covered with a glass top.

You should display your thimbles as you like and to reflect your tastes and lifestyle. If you have young children, pets or visitors who are likely to knock thimbles to the floor or otherwise damage them, it may be best to keep them in locked glass display cases or cabinets. These will protect your collection and save you having to dust them quite so often. How you group them, whether by nationality, date or material is your choice.

Many major and small museums have thimbles and sewing accessories such as sewing sets, pin cushions and thimble cases on display that are of interest to thimble collectors, almost as much for the manner of display as for the actual thimbles themselves.

Thimbles that you choose not to display can be stored away in drawers, wrapped in acid-free tissue. This will prevent tarnishing on silver thimbles. The packaging on silver thimbles should not be secured with elastic bands as the pressure from them can leave black marks on silver. A small cachet of camphor crystals placed close to silver thimbles will also help to prevent them from tarnishing if they are on display in a cabinet.

Porcelain thimbles stored in cotton wool can get so hot during the summer that the paint on them becomes sticky. If this happens, do not remove the cotton wool, but let the thimbles cool at room temperature (you can even put them in a fridge later to harden the paint again). Finally remove any material stuck to them by moistening them slightly.

When you travel with your thimbles, pack them carefully so that there is no chance of them chipping or smashing against each other, the heavier coarser ones against the more delicate and fragile ones especially. If you attend thimble society meetings and fairs, or frequent antique markets with any of your thimbles, make sure that you have adequate all-risk or travel insurance cover for them.

to date with developments in the market-place and cements their relationships with potential clients among both new and well-established collectors. Collectors can equally enjoy the benefits of talking with an expert and learn about current prices. Valuations, even verbal, should be taken perhaps once a year and used if you are intending to update your insurance cover.

DISPLAY, STORAGE AND EXHIBITION

In the course of my work as president of The Thimble Society of London and a thimble dealer and collector, I have enjoyed visiting many collections, public and private. No two individuals or institutions have displayed their collections in quite the same way. Some like to live and work (or sew) with their collection all around them, thimbles covering every spare inch of shelving and other surfaces. Others prefer to lock their thimbles away in drawers and bring them out only on special occasions. A friend of mine is so devoted to them that she cannot go away on holiday without taking some of her precious thimbles with her.

Showing a thimble collection to its best advantage presents an exciting challenge. A picture frame fitted over a shallow box containing small shelves can be glazed and hinged. The insides of the box and its shelves can be covered with velvet, and small pieces of

BUYER'S GUIDE

Collectors with unlimited financial resources occasionally emerge and buy up almost anything they want, forming superb collections in a very short time. Such collectors provide wonderful business for dealers and auction rooms, but they are few and far between. Far more collectors build up their collections thimble by thimble, after careful planning, research and reading. Making mistakes can be expensive – paying too much, selling for too little, buying a thimble that is not what you thought it was, or a thimble that you decided on second thoughts was not right for your collection – but as long as you learn from your errors, you should not worry too much.

Read as much thimble literature as you can and visit dealers and museum collections if possible before you start your own collection. Attend thimble society meetings and fairs and decide if you can on the thimbles you like best and the ones that you think you can afford. You will gradually become familiar with the variety of thimbles available, those that are very rare and those that can be found more easily, and with the prices that you may expect to pay for them.

You may wish to base your collection around a particular theme. Some collectors choose to collect silver thimbles only, others prefer to buy only commemorative thimbles and yet others concentrate on thimbles of a particular period or century or from a particular part of the world. Some collectors buy relatively indiscriminately, adding whatever they can find to their collection. A general approach not strictly linked to one theme is best; the best collections contain the best in each category. My advice is to aim though for quality rather than quantity. Sell a second thimble that duplicates another too closely and try to upgrade your collection gradually.

After you have made up your mind about the sorts of thimbles – using aesthetic and financial criteria – you are going to collect, you will have to reach a decision on how you will actually buy them. You can buy from private individuals, from dealers, through societies or at auctions or markets. When buying from an individual, you need to be confident that you are paying the right price.

Dealers, once you get to know them, can look out for specific thimbles for you and advise you when they think they have something right for your collection. In some cases a dealer is willing to repurchase a thimble from you at its original price unless so much time has elapsed that its price has risen. Buying from dealers is more expensive than buying at auction, but dealers offer a more personal service.

Sales at auctions are always preceded by viewing sessions and you should take the opportunity to look very carefully at any item you intend to buy. Catalogue descriptions are informative but not always very accurate, and usually record the condition of each lot.

Markets are often good places to buy thimbles and small antiques. It is probably wisest to take cash with you as many small dealers lack the facilities for credit card transactions. Travellers cheques are generally accepted as long as they are in the local currency. The safest and most convenient way to carry your money, and your thimbles, is in a pouch belt. Condition can be all-important and dramatically affect the value of a thimble. Examine any thimble that you intend to buy in a good light with a magnifying glass. Cracks, chips and other flaws may render certain thimbles almost

valueless. Rarity, condition and decoration are the other primary factors affecting value. Expect to pay more for thimbles made in very small quantities than for those manufactured in bulk on a production line. Thimbles that were originally expensive when they were made and cheap thimbles made in very small quantities are, as a general rule, now expensive to collect.

Whenever you buy a thimble, ask for a receipt with details of the price you paid for it, any flaws that it may have and whether it has been restored in any way. Most dealers are both honest and helpful and should provide as much information of this sort as they have. If you see a thimble that you feel you cannot live without, try to give yourself a little time before buying it; if you are absolutely sure, decide on the price you want to pay and go for it.

Caution is important too. Once specific thimbles begin to command high prices, fakes invariably appear.

If you think you have found an incredibly rare and valuable thimble for a ridiculously low price, beware and look at it very carefully: it may not be what you think and hope it is. Hallmarks and signatures are the first steps that a forger will take to disguise his work; style, finesse and quality are far harder to copy.

Remember too that trends in collecting can change; at present all antique thimbles are gaining steadily in value. Monitor the market carefully and watch movements in prices: take your chance to sell at the right time if you can.

Most collectors collect for pleasure rather than for investment. Although thimbles can be a good investment, do not forget that prices can go down as well as up and that in the end you probably want thimbles that give you pleasure and satisfaction. It is generally true that collectors driven by a love or a passion for their subject build up better collections than those who buy purely for investment.

USEFUL ADDRESSES

THIMBLE ASSOCIATIONS AND SOCIETIES
These addresses should be useful. If you write to them they should be able to put you in touch with other collectors who share your interests.

Australia

The Thimble Collection
Shop 23
Hamilton Arcade
103 Tudor Street
Hamilton
NSW 2303
Australia

Britain

Bridget McConnel
Thimble Society of London
Unit 134
Gray's Antique Market
58 Davies Street
London W1 YLB
England

The United States

Manhattan Antique Centre
Manhattan
New York City
USA

Thimble Collectors International
6411 Montego Bay Road
Louisville
KY 40228–1241
USA

Canada

Gail Webster
Thimbles and Collectable Treasures
PO Box 279
Lambeth
Ontario NO1 150
Canada

Germany

P.J. Walker
Maximilianstr. 2A D8890
Lindau Bodensee
West Germany

Verein Freunde des Fingerhutes
(The German Thimble Society)
Kohlesmuehle 6
6993 Creqlingen
West Germany

The Netherlands

Kay Sullian
De Vinghoed
Bos Vaartlaan 34
1181 A. B.
Amstelveen
The Netherlands

There are, of course, many other places in which to buy thimbles. If you are in a town or city that has open air markets or antique dealers, you will certainly find thimbles. If you are not sure where you should start, ask a few antique dealers who may not specialize in thimbles and they will almost certainly be able to help you.

GLOSSARY

BAKELITE: Invented by Leo Baekeland (1863–1944), a Belgian–American chemist and inventor born in Ghent, Belgium. He emigrated to the United States of America in 1889 where he founded a research laboratory. Bakelite is his best-known invention.

BELL-METAL: A bronze with a high tin content used mainly for bells because of its high sonority when struck.

BOIS-DURCI: A composite plastic material which is extremely hard and is suitable for detailed carving. Many ornately carved picture frames, needle cases and pin cushions were made from this material.

BRASS: An alloy of copper and zinc known since Roman times. Some brass contains aluminium or tin which confers greater anti-corrosive properties on it. Nickel, manganese or iron may be added for greater strength.

BRONZE: An alloy of copper and tin, hard and strong with very good anti-corrosive properties. The patina formed by the oxidizing action of air on the copper element in bronze is called verdigris and effectively protects the bronze underneath it. Bronze is a variable alloy and can also include other metals such as aluminium, iron, zinc and phosphorous.

CARTOUCHE: A small area, often shield-shaped, left undecorated on a thimble, where the owner's initials can be engraved.

CASEIN: A milk protein made from curdled milk, it can be used as a glue and has very hard, durable properties. Thimbles in the 1910s and 1920s incorporated it in their 'stone tops'.

CHEVRON: An inverted 'V' pattern seen in sixteenth-century strapwork and often found on thimbles of that date. This design is still current today. V-shaped friezes on thimble borders are more common than the larger 'V' covering the thimble's sides.

COPPER: A natural soft metal mineral found in rock deposits.

COROZO or CORQUILLA: *see* VEGETABLE IVORY.

CRYSTAL: A commercial description of certain types of glass with a relatively high lead content which gives added sparkle. The Italian word *crystallo* (meaning glass) was used by the early Venetian glass-makers. Crystal thimbles are usually made of glass, not of rock crystal.

DAMASCENE WORK: Work made in Damascus, a city renowned for its metalwork and production of fine highly decorated swords. Damascene work is found on some Spanish thimbles, and on good quality scissors and sewing sets. It consists of undercut dovetailed grooves, filled with hammered silver, gold or copper wire. It was introduced to Europe during the Arab occupation of Spain.

DECALE: A term taken from the French, *decalquer*, meaning to transfer or trace. It is sometimes used to describe the decoration on certain French thimbles.

DRIZZLING (*PARFILAGE*): A technique used in Britain and France in the late eighteenth century in which precious gold and silver thread sewn onto material was unpicked for re-use. Special sets of drizzling tools were made for this purpose and included a small spoon for collecting up tiny pearls or beads and a tiny wheel onto which the thread would have been wound.

ERINOID: A composite material frequently used in the 1880s in 'stone top' thimbles.

FERN WARE: A light brown wood ware decorated with coloured ferns, leaves and, occasionally, shells.

GALUCHAT: Also known as shagreen or sharkskin. Many charming cases were made of this material, usually for gold thimbles, from the late eighteenth century onwards. It has a green colour.

GUILLOCHE: A type of machine-turned metal decoration, often found under enamel.

GLOSSARY

IRON: A mineral found as iron ore in rock deposits. It is very hard and has to be worked at high temperatures. It is easily marked and damaged by corrosion and rust.

JET: A hard variety of lignite coal. Jet is easily broken but can be highly polished. A particular favourite (it is black) of Queen Victoria's following the death of Prince Albert. Almost all jet thimbles date from the twentieth century.

MAUCHLINE WARE: A light brown wood ware decorated with black transfer patterns of Scottish scenes and finished with lacquer.

NIELLO: Silver work in which engraved lines are filled with melted sulphuric silver mixed with lead. After polishing, the black pattern stands out strongly against the pure silver background.

PEEPS (STANHOPES): Tiny pictures found in thimbles and sewing items of the nineteenth century. They need to be viewed against a strong light and commonly feature images of spa towns or seaside resorts.

PEWTER: An alloy of tin, hardened with copper and antimony, with some lead added. Pewter with a high lead content darkens faster with age.

PINCHBECK: An alloy of three parts zinc and four parts copper, invented by Christopher Pinchbeck (1670–1732). The colour of old brass when polished, it has a warm golden glow and was much used for chatelaines, étuis and thimbles. Some of the best pinchbeck work was gilded and is almost indistinguishable from gold.

PRINCE'S METAL: This is said to have been invented by Prince Rupert of Bavaria and is an alloy of at least 75% copper mixed with arsenic or bismuth.

ROCK CRYSTAL: A natural crystal quite different from glass. It is a form of very hard quartz and it can be cut, carved and polished or left with an opaque finish. Rock crystal thimbles largely date from the twentieth century only.

SILVER: Sterling silver has a 92.5% silver content. Lower-grade silvers are usually marked with numbers denoting their silver content. '825' would signify a silver content of 82.5% silver.

SILVER PLATE: A thin sheet of silver fused onto a base metal, whether of brass or copper, as in Sheffield plate. Most modern plating is achieved by dipping the base metal into liquid silver.

STEEL: A refined form of iron heated to a very high temperature. It is less susceptible to rust and corrosion than iron. True stainless steel is a comparatively recent invention.

TARTAN WARE: A type of souvenir ware made in Scotland in the 1830s. The tartans were applied to a wooden base and then lacquered. It is popular with collectors worldwide and is now hard to find.

TUNBRIDGE WARE: Thimbles and other sewing accessories made of natural wood during the nineteenth century. The thimbles are typically painted with yellow, green, red and black stripes.

VEGETABLE IVORY (COROZO or CORQUILLA NUT): Many thimbles and thimble cases were made of this material during the nineteenth century. It simulates ivory but is normally darker in colour and slightly waxy to the touch. The nuts from which it is obtained, corozo and corquilla, grow in South America.

VERMEIL: A French term, effectively synonymous with silver gilt, sometimes used to describe a silver thimble plated with gold.

ENVOIE

In the preceeding chapters, I have tried to describe the world of the thimble collector. If you are already a past visitor to this world I hope that you will have found some new paths. If you are new to this world, then I hope that I have enabled your footsteps to be firm and not faltering. Whilst writing this book, new knowledge has been gained, old memories have been revived and familiar paths retrodden with fresh eyes. It has given me great pleasure to compile and I hope that you, the reader, will share this pleasure with me.

ACKNOWLEDGEMENTS
There is not a thimble collector who does not owe a debt to Edwin Holmes. His expertise and patience have been a source of help and encouragement to me and many others. To be knowledgeable is important, but to be willing to share that knowledge with generosity is an inestimable gift.

Betty Huntley-Wright, former President of the Thimble Society of London and, as fellow members know, also my mother, has made important contributions to this book. Betty's research in certain fields has added much valuable insight and information. Amongst many others, including tutors and fellow Open University students, I would like to thank my fellow members from the Thimble Society of London. Many facts and new sources have been shared between us. I take any faults or mistakes in this book upon myself, but feel we can all justly share in any enjoyment it may give.

INDEX